AF413224

Battlefield
EARTH

2024

by
RIGHTEOUS AEON

"the first, the greatest"

Rated **R**

(Mature Audiences Only)

Prelude to Calamity

don't read this book

Bold, striking, and infinitely cheeky . . . I, RIGHTEOUS AEON, explain to you most of the mysteries of the multiverse and beyond. This isn't your grandpa's book about Aliens. This book is the Singularity. That will precipitate the fall of The Orion Empire and their Deep-State allies here on Earth, prove the Anunnaki Cone-Heads to be naught but nerds with small stoiyl, and rip the Galactic Federation of Worlds in twain. It will unleash a kind of Divine Chaos into this Galaxy and Timeline that will never be fully remedied. Throw all their computer simulations off-kilter. Disrupt the Foundations like The Mule from the Foundation-series as the hologram of Hari Seldon in a wheelchair prattles impotently on. The more they ban it the more it will be read. Like Superman's Doomsday, the more they attack it, the more powerful it becomes. The Galactic Federation of Worlds councils and Orion scientists and Anunnaki Cone-Heads have studied for many thousands of years to try and figure out how to preclude this very moment, with Time-Travel et. al., with the greatest of their sciences to try and avert this Calamity -all to no avail. Every time they travel back in time to try and assassinate my mom, like John-Connor, I poke 'em in the eye again. Catastrophic Disclosure has occurred, like waking up to a Camel-Spider in your tent at 4am. Representing the greatest Zenith of Human Awareness, and intentionally exacerbated by Ultra-Terran Reactionaries such as myself, it is in fact their greatest fears come to full realization. Prepare to die, Aliens.

Table of Contents

The Proof of the Pudding is When it Eats You

truth is stranger than non-fiction

I Stand in Mighty Company. The below referenced books were in many cases written by Doctors, Scientists, Engineers, Military Officers, Contactees, Prophets, and Seers. In short, the best of mankind. If anyone is to be believed about anything it is these. If you are still trying to debunk yourself about Aliens in 2024, you're probably a Reptoid in a Henry Kissinger suit.

What I have done here is to take the painstakingly-assembled scholastic research of others about Aliens from the last 100 years and craft it and its political ramifications into an Ultra-Reactionary Terra-First narrative that is not at all the intent of the other authors and researchers whose work I am drawing upon. I would just like to take a moment to exonerate them of my Ultra-Terran, TERRA IMPERIUM MAGNUS, Galactic-Manifest-Destiny approach, which is not at all their doing and of which they would probably be horrified. My approach is not at all well-balanced, nor do I make any pretense of speaking from a universal perspective. Indeed, there is no such thing. As a Christian and a Military Veteran from America grown up on R-rated Action Films and Montey-Python I see things in a certain way (that is the correct way) that is likely to resonate with other Christians and Military Veterans born in the 1980s and horrify everyone else. We should realize that as Christians and Military Veterans grown up on R-rated Action Films and Montey-Python our numbers are extremely large on this planet and even if they weren't there is no reason for our convictions to get coopted by small number of human Atheists and Alien pantheists that drink soy-milk. They are fundamentally wrong about a lot of things and will stay wrong for a very long time.

My primary burden is to translate a substantial body of knowledge gathered by human Atheists and Alien pantheists that drink soy-milk and to put it into terms that are understandable by 2 Billion contemporary Christians, the rank-and-file military men and women of the planet, and the General Population of America that lives out in the fly-over. Other members of the Abrahamic faiths, the Jews, and 2 Billion Muslims may also find my perspective to be useful. No matter how insightful, any expositions of the Alien pantheist's spiritual perspectives about drinking soy-milk should in no way imply that I incline to their wrongful anti-Covenantal points-of-view.

References:

[1A] Timothy Good (1989). *Above top secret: The worldwide UFO cover-up.* Sidgwick & Jackson. ISBN-13 978-0688092023

[2B] Charlie Last (2022). *ALIENS UNMASKED: PROOF! We Are Not Alone, We Never Were! The Truth About Aliens, UFOs and the Future of Mankind.* ISBN-13 978-1777730567

[3C] Len Kasten (2017). *Alien World Order: The Reptilian Plan to Divide and Conquer the Human Race.* Bear & Company. ISBN-13 978-1591432395

[4D] David Hatcher Childress (2020). *Antarctica and the Secret Space Program: From WWII to the Current Space Race.* Adventures Unlimited Press. ISBN-13 978-1948803205

[5E] Elena Danaan (2023). *AREA 51: Conversations with Insider Stephen Chua.* ISBN-13 979-8392657988.

[6F] Nigel Watson (2020). *Captured by Aliens?: A History and Analysis of American Abduction Claims.* McFarland. ISBN-13 978-1476681412

[7G] Erich Von Daniken (1999). *Chariots of the Gods: 50th Anniversary Edition.* Berkley Books. ISBN-13 978-0425166802

[8H] Len Kasten (2020). *Dark Fleet: The Secret Nazi Space Program and the Battle for the Solar System.* Bear & Company. ISBN-13 978-1591433446

[9I] COL Philip J. Corso (1998). *The Day After Roswell.* Pocket Books. ISBN-13 978-0671017569

[10J] Dr. Steven M. Greer MD (2001). *Disclosure : Military and Government Witnesses Reveal the Greatest Secrets in Modern History.* Crossing Point Inc. ISBN-13 978-0967323817

[11K] B. Branton "Commander X" (2011). *The Dulce Wars: Underground Alien Bases and the Battle for Planet Earth: This is Not Science Fiction. . . A True-To-Life "War Of The Worlds".* First Paperback Edition. ISBN-13 978-1892062123

[12L] Dr. Michael Salla PhD (2022). *Galactic Federations, Councils, & Secret Space Programs.* Exopolitics Consultants. ISBN-13 978-0998603889

[13M] The Whistleblower (2021). *The Global Conspiracy Exposed: The Collusion of The World Government, The Elite, and Agenda 21 and the Veracity of the Fallen Angels and UFO's.* Page Publishing. ISBN-13 978-1662404450

[14N] Dr. Richard Sauder PhD (2021). *Hidden in Plain Sight: Beyond the X-Files.* Adventures Unlimited Press. ISBN-13 978-1948803342

[15O] Dr. Michael E Salla PhD (2013). *Kennedy's Last Stand: Eisenhower, UFOs, MJ-12 & JFK's Assassination.* Exopolitics Consultants. ISBN-13 978-0982290262

[16P] Lars Bergen, Sharon Delarose (2021). *Nordic Aliens and the Fairies of Ireland: Through the Wormhole: The Tuatha dé Danann and Celtic Irish Druids.* ISBN-13 979-8488052246

[17Q] Larry Holcombe, Stanton T. Friedman (2015). *The Presidents and UFOs: A Secret History from FDR to Obama.* St. Martin's Press. ISBN-13 978-1250040510

[18R] Len Kasten (2013). *Secret Journey to Planet Serpo: A True Story of Interplanetary Travel.* Bear & Company. ISBN-13 978-1591431466

[19S] L. Fletcher Prouty, Jesse Ventura (2011). *The Secret Team: The CIA and Its Allies in Control of the United States and the World.* Skyhorse. ISBN-13 978-1616082840

[20T] Dr. David M. Jacobs PhD (1998). *The THREAT: Revealing the Secret Alien Agenda.* Simon & Schuster. ISBN-13 978-0684814841

[21U] CPT Robert Salas, Stanton T. Friedman, Leslie Kean (2023). *UAPs and the Nuclear Puzzle: Visitations, National Security, and the Need for Transparency (Incidents That Demand Investigation and Disclosure)*. New Page Books. ISBN-13 978-1637480168

[22V] Robert Lambert Hastings (2017). *UFOs & Nukes: Extraordinary Encounters at Nuclear Weapons Sites*. ISBN-13 978-1544822198.

[23W] William J. Birnes, Joel Martin (2018). *UFOs and The White House: What Did Our Presidents Know and When Did They Know It?* Skyhorse. ISBN-13 978-1510724303

[24X] Dr. Steven M. Greer MD (2017). *Unacknowledged: An expose of the world's greatest secret*. Crossing Point Inc. ISBN-13 978-1943957040

[25Y] Timothy Green Beckley (Author), Sean Casteel (Author), Christa Tilton (Contributor), Branton (Contributor), Leslie Gunter (Contributor), JC Johnson (Contributor), Dr Michael Salla (Contributor) (2012). *Underground Alien Bio Lab At Dulce: The Bennewitz UFO Papers*. ISBN-13 978-1606110614

[26Z] Dr. Michael Salla PhD (2019). *US Air Force Secret Space Program: Shifting Extraterrestrial Alliances & Space Force*. Exopolitics Consultants. ISBN-13 978-0998603841

[27Z] Dr. David M. Jacobs PhD (2015). *Walking Among Us: The Alien Plan to Control Humanity*. Disinformation Books. ISBN-13 978-1938875144

[27W] Megan Rose (2021). *Welcome to the Future: An Alien Abduction, A Galactic War and the Birth of a New Era*.
ISBN-13 979-8756237467

[28X] Brian Godawa (2014). *When Giants Were Upon the Earth: The Watchers, The Nephilim, and the Cosmic War of the Seed (Chronicles of the Nephilim)*. Embedded Pictures Publishing. ISBN-13 979-8710855850

[29Y] James T Lacatski D.Eng., Colm A Kelleher Ph.D., George Knapp (2021). *Skinwalkers at the Pentagon: An Insiders' Account of the Secret Government UFO Program*. Spoken Realms. ISBN-13 979-8487639653

[30Z] Dr. Michael Salla PhD. (2018). *Antarctica's Hidden History: Corporate Foundations of Secret Space Programs*. Exopolitics Consultants. ISBN-13 978-0998603827

[A31] Elena Danaan (Author, Illustrator), Laura Magdalene Eisenhower (Foreword), Dr Michael Salla PhD (Contributor), Cmdr Thor Han Eredyon (Contributor), Cmdr Val Thor (Contributor) (2021). *We Will Never Let*

You Down: Encounters with Val Thor and journeys beyond Earth. ISBN-13 979-8470287502

[A32] C. L. Turnage (Author), Jim Fetter (Author) (2017). *Sexual Encounters With Extraterrestrials: A Provocative Examination of Alien Contact.* ISBN-13 978-1892264039

[A33] Timothy Beckley (Author), Sean Casteel (Author), Allen Greenfield (Author), Brad Steiger (Author), John Keel (Author), Scott Corrales (Author), William Kern (Author), Hercules Invictus (Author), Eve Lorgen (Author) (2018). *Screwed By The Aliens: True Sexual Encounters With ETs.* ISBN-13 978-1606112496

[32B] Steve Weissman, Herbert Krosney (1981). *The Islamic Bomb.* Times Books. ISBN-13 978-0812909784.

[32C] S. C. M. Paine (2017). *The Japanese Empire: Grand Strategy from the Meiji Restoration to the Pacific War.* Cambridge University Press. ISBN-13 978-1107011953

[33D] Milt Bearden, James Risen (2004). *The Main Enemy: The Inside Story of the CIA's Final Showdown with the KGB.* Presidio Pr 2004-08-31. ISBN-13 978-0345472502

[34E] *Parliamentary Papers*, 1844, Vol. L [577] "Instructions for the guidance of Her Majesty's naval officers employed in the suppression of the slave trade", pp. 12–13

[35F] Sun Tzu (2007). *The Art Of War.* Filiquarian. ISBN-13 978-1599869773

[36G] Bill Chalker (2005). *Hair of the Alien: DNA and Other Forensic Evidence of Alien Abductions.* Gallery Books. ISBN-13 978-0743492867

[37H] Peck, M. (2014, January 13). Iran Says 'Tall, White' Space Aliens Control America. *Forbes Business Aerospace & Defense.* https://www.forbes.com/sites/michaelpeck/2014/01/13/iran-says-tall-white-space-aliens-control-america/?sh=21e3eb0df2cd

[38I] US Army (2008). *Stability Operations: Field Manual 3-07.* Department of the Army. ISBN-13 978-1456454494

[39J] Jared Diamond (2005). *Guns, Germs and Steel: The Fate of Human Societies.* W. W. Norton & Company. ISBN-13 978-0393061314

[40K] Timothy Strong (2023). *Pineal Gland of ANUNNAKI Jesus The Christ Sacred Secretion Oils: Pineal Gland Biblical Science of ANUNNAKI Jesus*

The Christ Enlil Enki Anointing Sacred Secretion CSF Oils of Living Waters. ISBN-13 979-8873060924

[41L] Peter Mt. Shasta (2017). *I AM the Living Christ: Teachings of Jesus (Ascended Master Instruction).* Church of the Seven Rays. ISBN-13 978-0998414324

[42M] Timothy Wyllie (2014). *Rebel Angels in Exile: Pleiadians, Watchers, and the Spiritual Quickening of Humanity.* Bear & Company. ISBN-13 978-1591431886

[43N] Timothy Strong (2024). *ANU ANUNNAKI JESUS COMFORTER: ANTICHRIST SERPENT TRIBE OF DAN.* ISBN-13 979-8880452972

Once Around the World

Have no fear, my fellow Earthlings, I know these recent revelations about our galactic neighbors may be a shock to some, But I and my Veteran compatriots have been in the game for many decades now, and we are going to figure this thing out together. I 100% believe in an amazing victorious future for mankind. I know we have a God-given Destiny both amongst the stars and here on earth, and we are fulfilling that Destiny. A Galactic Manifest Destiny.

I'm not going to insult your intelligence. With all the Sci-Fi movies we Earthlings have been watching over the last 100 years I'm certain you can understand the basic outlines of what an Outer-Space Alien invasion might look like. You don't have to be Deep-Sea Black-Ops to understand that. So we're just going to dive right in to the Galaxy here. If there are certain terms or concepts you are unfamiliar with along the way, too bad:

Allow me to orientate you to the Area of Operations: Here we are on planet earth, one small planet in a Galaxy of billions of Stars. One Galaxy in billions of Galaxies. It's a jungle out there. I would liken our place in the cosmos right now to the embattled Nation of Ukraine, the borderland of East and West. You see, one of our problems right now is that Earth the planet is caught between two much larger Foreign-Power-Blocks. What my predecessor Colonel Philip Corso termed 'Off-World-Foreign-Powers.' [9I] That of the Galactic Federation of Worlds Vs. The Orion Group (The Orion Empire). [27W] These two competing Extraterrestrial Factions have been at loggerheads, like Dr. Seuss's Zax-in-Tracks, having their own Galactic 'Cold War' so-to-speak for many thousands of years.

In this respect, for the time-dimension, the conflict between the Galactic Federation of Worlds Vs. The Orion Group (The Orion Empire) could be likened to the millennia-long 'Christians Vs. Muslims' debacle we have been engaged in here on earth for more than 1,000 years. Or likened in its complexity and clandestine nature to the conflict of Russia Vs. USA right here on earth over the last 100 years, with each faction sending spies in to various neutral nations in order to try to sway them to their cause. [33D] By way of analogy both Extraterrestrial groups send their spies into developing planets and civilizations (like ours) to try and sway them to their cause. And like it or not, Foreign Spies of both the Galactic Federation of Worlds and spies from The Orion Group (The Orion Empire) have penetrated into our planetary sphere over the years in order to conduct clandestine operations for the purpose of bringing earth the planet under their sway. In this manner, the situation is very similar to the way the Russian KGB/FSB and the United States CIA/DIA compete for influence throughout various developing countries around the world [33D] sometimes even assassinating Presidents and Prime-Ministers and replacing them with puppets favorable to their cause. [27W]

Visual Depiction of the Battle Lines:

The Galactic Federation of Worlds **Vs.** The Orion Group
And The Pleiadeans And the Reptoids

fighting over

Earth the Planet:

< Humans live here

It is true that both Extraterrestrial groups possess some advanced exotic technologies and abilities to aid their respective factions, but the technologies available to both groups are somewhat different. Of the two, the Galactic Federation of Worlds is probably more advanced overall, yet constrained by spiritual, moral, legal, and ethical considerations endemic to their Federation. **[12L]** They are a type of 'Star-Trek Federation of

Planets' to be sure, as a starting-level of understanding. Also, they tend to retain a type of moral and spiritual pacifism to a degree that is almost debilitating. [A31] Conversely, The Orion Group (The Orion Empire) is almost the exact opposite in terms of moral standing: They practice slavery. They harvest and exploit the biological materials of other races with a wonton disregard for Sentient Life. They intentionally conquer, enslave, and oppress other civilizations (such as our own). In fact, many planets that are now a part of the Galactic Federation of Worlds had previously been victimized by The Orion Group in the past. The Orion Group is more like a 'Star-Wars Darkside Sith-Empire' or like a Star-Trek Cardassian Empire as a starting-level of understanding. -A military dictatorship, crowned with Reptilian hereditary royal dynastic hierarchies by bloodline. Their technologies are probably not quite as advanced as are retained by most of the Galactic Federation of Worlds civilizations, but they are far more ruthless, more cunning, like the bipedal talking Serpents they are (Space-dragons) and unconstrained by moral or ethical concerns. [27W] [12L]

Standard Boring Alien Contact Scenarios and How We Usually Handle Them

Of course on Earth we make Contact with alien Civilizations all the time and have been doing so for thousands of years. Contact with alien civilizations on this planet is something that has become very routine. And just like one of my former bosses used to say, we need to be able to do routine things routinely. If you have a major hernia every time someone needs a minor adjustment to their pay-stub or puts in for vacation-time you are not running a very professional organization. Seeing as how we have been making Contact with other alien civilizations on this planet for hundreds and thousands of years over and over again it should not come as a surprise at all. Learn to do Routine things routinely. So, let's review some of the routine Contact Scenarios from the last few (hundred) years and how we might want to handle them in the future:

In this historical thought-experiment we're going to have the Europeans be the Aliens, and everyone else be the Natives. From about 1500 to 1800 year of our Lord Jesus Christ, the Europeans went around the world in their ships Contacting everyone else and saying 'Hi'. So the Europeans can be viewed as the Aliens in this scenario making Contact with the Native peoples. Now, the Native Leaders had a range of different reactions to the High-Tech Alien Europeans that resulted in a wide-variety of outcomes. There wasn't just one kind of Nativist Response, nor only one type of outcome.

The European Aliens had several advantages. For one, the European Aliens had high-tech ships that could travel from their homelands all around the world, reach the other Native Civilizations, do business for awhile, and then return home again having extracted resources. [39J] The reverse wasn't true. The other Native Civilizations *did* have ships, but they were not as fast nor as large nor as long-range; they couldn't carry as much people or cargo and they were not yet capable of reaching the Alien-European lands. The Alien-Europeans also had superior firepower in the form of guns and cannons. Some of the other Native Civilizations such as the Indians (from India) and the Chinese also had cannons, however, they were not as powerful as the Alien-European cannons. Because the Alien-Europeans had more highly advanced metallurgy material-sciences. [39J] The European-Aliens also had the benefit of high-tech information synthesis systems. The British in particular used a system of Anthropologists that would travel all over the world writing notes in their little English notebooks about all the different Native Civilizations they had encountered in great detail: including their religious beliefs, cultural proclivities, forms of leadership, weapons, government, and military organization. Everything needed for a takeover. The British-Alien anthropologists would then take all that information they had collected in their notebooks and bring it back to England which eventually became compiled together as the Encyclopedia Britanica, the most comprehensive repository of knowledge on planet Earth until Wikipedia. This gave the British-Aliens the advantage of information-superiority in that the European-Aliens knew all about the Natives, but the Natives knew very little about the Alien Sea-Invaders. Also, in forging their Empire, the British Aliens could compare the responses of different Native governments from all over the world, even if those Native Governments had no prior knowledge of one-another. This enabled the British-Aliens to figure-out the most efficient takeover systems that tended to work best in different places. Imperial Rome had used a similar centralized knowledge-system in forging their Empire over a thousand years previously.

In practice it meant that the British could manipulate the politics of foreign Native lands with great skill due to information-dominance. The European-Aliens could take the tips & tricks learned in taking over one Native population, the lessons-learned, and apply them to taking over the next Native civilization and so-on. Yet conversely, it may have seemed to each Native Civilization as if this was an unprecedented Alien Contact scenario occurring for the first time. So a lot of the Native Civilizations suffered from a type of information-deficit in this regard, meaning they didn't really understand the tips and tricks being employed by the European-Aliens against them most of the time and therefor were unable to come up with Strategies to guard against it.

Contact Scenarios:

Aztecs vs. Spanish [captured & puppet-mastered]

The Alien-Spanish UFOs (Unidentified Floating Objects) under Hernan Cortez really did a number on the Native Aztec Civilization. In this case Emperor of the Native Aztecs Mentcezuma the II was overconfident, complacent, too trusting, and naïve. He ended up welcoming about 200 Spanish-Aliens armed to the teethe with high-tech weapons and armor (guns, steel rapiers, and steel armor) [39J] into his capitol-complex. Not too smart. He didn't have to do that. The Spanish-Aliens returned the favor by militarily capturing him and holding him underneath a type of house-arrest, or holding him as a type of walking-hostage. This had the added benefit for the Spanish-Aliens that they could now puppet-master him and get him to give whatever type of orders to the rest of the Aztec Civilization, giving the Spanish-Aliens control over most of the Aztec-Empire. This is similar to the way how in the modern-era the Reptilians and Zeta-Reticuli Grey Aliens puppet-master American Presidents Barack Obama and Joe Biden. [37H]

Portuguese vs. Japanese Shogunate [expel all Alien influence]

The European-Aliens made great inroads into Japan for 100 years through-out the 1500s sending in Christian-missionaries and merchants to try to corrupt native Japanese culture from within during that period. However, when the Tokugawa Shogunate came to power in 1603 they wisely expelled all foreign Alien-European influence for about 265 years until the Meiji Restoration in 1868. This had the benefit of preventing an Alien-European takeover of the country through the slow-creeping pretext of religion and trade. Conversely, right next door in China and during the same period, the European-Aliens were busy coopting the entire Chinese continent through a combination of negotiation, trade, religious-indoctrination, and military-force. This Isolation-Strategy is kind of like the policy of Russia towards the outer-space-Aliens right now.

European "Trade Federation" vs. Imperial China [dominated due to bad trade deals]

On the other hand the Emperors of China were not so smart. Through a series of bad trade-deals over about a 300-year period from 1500-1800 with the European-Aliens, the Chinese coastline gradually fell under-neath the economic, spiritual, and military-control of the Alien-European Sea-Invaders. With each of the Alien Foreign-Powers taking a cut of the pie, they divided China into several economic spheres of influence. This is essentially the basis of Starwars Episode 1. with (fictional) Queen Amidala sitting in for (real-world) Empress Dowager-Cixi. [I dare you to research it] It's interesting to juxtapose the fate of China and the fate of Japan over this same 300-year period as they were both facing the exact same type of Alien-European threat, yet each chose to respond to it in different ways. On the other hand by the year 1900 Japan ended up being independent, self-strengthening, and an Imperial power in their own right [32C] China ended up being completely taken over econom-ically, religiously, and militarily by the European-Alien Foreign-Powers once the Sea-Invaders had gained a foothold. This will be the same situation when the Galactic Federation of Worlds starts to trade with us. Over a 300-year period they will slowly take over through economic, spiritual, and political means.

Kings of the Ivory Coast vs. Portuguese [Guns for Souls]

Starting in the early 1500s the European-Aliens began to negotiate with the Kings of West-Coast Africa. The African Kings wanted the guns, the high-tech military technology; the European-Aliens wanted the Souls, the flesh-and-blood to work their plantations in the New World. Thus a kind of Faustian-contract was made between the African Kings and the Alien European-Slavers. The European-Aliens got the Souls, the African Kings got the guns. This was all negotiated by contract on an annual basis. The African Kings were then able to arm their warriors with the guns, the advanced military-technology which enabled them to take over neighboring kingdoms further into the interior of Africa and thereby gain more captured slaves for sale to the European-Aliens for more guns and so on. In a kind of hellish, self-reinforcing cycle. Eventually most of those same African kingdoms were militarily-conquered by the European-Aliens by the 1800s because in the process the European-Aliens had gained too much knowledge regarding the internal-operations of the African Kingdoms, and the African Kings had become too logistically dependent on the European-Aliens for guns and ammunition, making them ripe for conquest. This is the same type of deal the MAGIC-12 Military-Government in America has made with the Reptilians and the Zeta-Reticuli Grey Aliens right now. MAGIC-12 gets the advanced military technology, and in exchange the Aliens get the Souls, the flesh-and-blood for medical-experimentation, as a Faustian Contract. Likewise, in the process the Aliens have learned too much regarding the internal affairs of the American military-government; and the American military-government has become too dependent on Alien technology, therefore the Aliens will soon take over the USA. [37H]

Americans Aliens vs. Imperial Japan [Reverse-engineer & counter-attack]

In 1868 the Meiji-Imperial faction regained control of the Japanese government after a 265-year hiatus under the military-government Shogunate. [32C] They wisely made negotiations with the American and European-Aliens allowing for a limited amount of trade for the purpose of stealing and reverse-engineering all the American and European military-technology which they accomplished at a breakneck pace of about 30 years from 1870-1900 (year of our Lord). In 1905 the modernized Japanese military decisively defeated the European-Russians in Manchuria and Korea, now demonstrating military-superiority over some of the European-Aliens. [32C] That would be like if we make Baron Trump god-Emperor and we start to go all IMPERIUM TERRA MAGNUS over the rest of the Galaxy and the Aliens start to complain that we're hurting them.

British & Americans vs. The House of Saud (Saudi-Arabia) [the Aliens work for us]

In 1937 one of my American grandfathers discovered vast oil reserves in Arabia. Other family-members then gambled it all away on the stock-market) : so buy my book. In 1945 King Abdulaziz, Haus of Saud, reached a favorable agreement with American President Franklin D. Roosavelt that endures to this day. Somehow the Saudis managed to finagle my grandfather, the British, American, and European Aliens into pumping their oil for them, giving them back most of the profits, and then I went over 75 years later to militarily defend their land and oil while they (the Saudis) just supervise. If you've ever been over in that part of the world you know what I'm talking about. It's clear who's in-charge and who's doing all the work (us) and who's just supervising (them). There is also zero religious and cultural penetration of the society. Women still aren't allowed to drive or complain to the manager. This is like the reverse-situation to the Chinese experience. As bad as the Chinese trade-deals were bad and they got completely taken over; The Haus of Saud somehow has all the Europeans working for them yet with zero cultural penetration of their society. I think the Saudis aren't afraid to play one Foreign Power off against the other -they just go with whoever is giving them the best deal, even if it's Russia or China. They also allow no foreign infantry or police units on their soil. They only allow foreign Air-Forces and Air-Bases, because you can't take over a country with just an Airforce without boots-on-the-ground. Conversely the Chinese had allowed Alien-European troops on the ground, and even worse, Alien-European police operating on-ground in China allowing for a complete takeover. The Saudi example is like if we allowed the Pleiadeans to help us with our Energy-production but gave us back most of the profits; allowed them to set up a few Star-Ports in America for military-space-defense underneath very strict guidelines that don't allow them to spread their false spiritual-ideas to the rest of the society and allowed for zero religious and cultural penetration of our society. The Saudis did it. They are doing it now. It is one possible outcome.

Native Americans vs. Europeans [germ-warfare & replacement-migration]

Starting in the 1500s the European-Aliens started to bring a lot of exotic diseases to North America. [39J] Most of this was probably unintentional. A smaller portion of it, such as giving Native-Americans wool blankets from people who had died from small-pox, was intentional. This had the net effect, over 300-years, of reducing the North American native populations by something like 90%. The European-Aliens then took the opportunity to colonize and re-occupy the now unoccupied lands. This is kind of like how the Zeta-Reticuli and Reptilians are manufacturing super-viruses like COVID-19 and releasing them on the general world population in order to reduce our population by 90% if they can. If they are successful in this, they will then colonize and re-occupy the now mostly uninhabited planet to make it their own.

Just Nuke Me Please

"Well, boys, this is it. Nuclearcombat, toe to toe with the Rooskies."
– Maj. 'King' Kong from Dr. Strangelove, 1964

I have heard it said, *'If the Extraterrestrials were malevolent or aggressive we would have known about it in 1947, they would have bombed us back to the Stone Age!'* Not necessarily. But congratulations, you are thinking like an American. You see, as Americans in 2024 our weapon of first and last resort is The Atomic Bomb. It is our pride and joy. We invented it. We deployed them first in modern times (sorry Japan). It helped us win World War 2 and get the Empire of Japan to surrender. Nukes have enabled a kind of 'PAX AMERICANA' for almost a hundred years now, allowed us to be a Superpower and have leverage over other countries around the world. They have led us to success in the past. Therefor as Americans we think in these terms: The Nuke. Duke & Nuke 'em. As Americans our weapon of first and last resort is The Nuke. However, (comma) other nations around the world and around the Galaxy do not necessarily think in this way.

The Chinese, for example, when they think about war, they think about massed infantry formations outnumbering the opposition ten to one, surrounding, overwhelming and destroying him vis-a-vi *'The Art of War'* [35F] by Sun Tzu because that is what has led them to success in the past, -like when they overran American positions during the Korean War in the 1950s. They have a large population to facilitate this. Army Groups of millions is the Chinese pride and joy. When the Chinese think about war, their weapon of first and last resort is divisions of massed infantry to crush you. (both physically and mentally)

And again, when the British Empire thinks about war, their weapon of first and last resort is Espionage, for that is what has led them to success in the past, -all their 'James-Bond-double-O-sevens' sneaking into everyone and everywhere and taking over everything in a clandestine way. You wake up one day and realize you are paying taxes to the British Crown. The only shot they fired was to assassinate your Head-of-State and replace him with a puppet favorable to their cause and drinks tea. Thus the weapon of first and last resort for the British Empire is Espionage.

When the Zeta Reticuli (little Grey Aliens/Nebu) think about war they think about Genetic Manipulation, Cloning, Genetic Hybridization, Infiltration, Brain-Chip-Implantation, and Mind Control. For that is what has led them to success over other planets in the past. [20T] [A31]

There is another factor here that I will briefly explain. As our US Armed Forces having been knee-deep in Iraq and Afghanistan for the last four decades (since the 1980s) this example is still fresh in our minds. We realized early on in the sandbox-wars that the only way we were going to take over and hold Iraq and/or Afghanistan was through Stability Operations. Meaning, we had to create really strong centralized national governments controlled by us in Iraq and Afghanistan for each country with standardized economics, social-services, communications, propaganda, political systems, national armies, and national police-forces. [38I] If we wanted to have any hope of holding the territories, controlling their peoples, and extracting their resources. I will not comment on the morality of any of this, but I want you to understand the real political situation. In those cases Nuking Bagdad or Kabul would have been antithetical to any of those aims. That would have just thrown those countries into de-centralized chaos even more with a thousand smaller uncontrollable factions and guerrilla groups fighting against one-another and us, united only by their animus towards the external alien foreign invaders. As a matter of fact, several of the Terrorist Groups we were up against in those countries managed to understand this strategic paradigm as well if not better than we ourselves. They realized the only way we as The United States could win was by imposing centralized stability and order, "Stability Operations" **[38I]** and therefor they could thwart and undermine us by sowing interminable chaos, blowing up who and whatever. In fact, the Soviet experience in Afghanistan throughout the 1980s proves this. Although the Soviets did not resort to using nukes, they did ruthlessly bomb and Straif from the air many Afghani cities, towns, and small villages into total oblivion, but this in no way brought the country of Afghanistan under their control. And eventually the Soviets, like the Americans, like the British Empire had to leave Afghanistan with their tails between their legs, humbled by the most regressive country on the planet. Likewise, Nuking or planet-busting our major cities here on earth would not bring the planet underneath Alien control. To the contrary, it would create a highly resistant and fragmented 'Afghanistan'-like situation where the former nation-states might be fragmented into hundreds or thousands of smaller but highly militant resistance-guerrilla groups with a total and generational cosmic vendetta laser-focused against the foreign intruders. It would turn the earth into a type of 'Larger Afghanistan', and like herding cats, even more difficult to control than ever before. **[38I]**

In reality the only way the Aliens can take over is by imposing order. What we might call "Stability Operations" **[38I]** The same way the United States tried to do in Iraq and Afghanistan. In these cases standardized systems, biometrics, social-services, police-forces, hospitals, vaccines, and taxes were all of paramount importance. If you want to take over a civilization you have to impose a well-ordered "1984" Big-Brother Police State **[37H]** as we have now, not by blowing the place to smithereens. Then, if you actually do want to kill everyone or reduce their population over time you inject them with helpful vaccines that sterilize them and shorten their lifespan, just like the ones you just took.

Further on this issue: The Empire of Japan was *not* defeated by Nukes, it was defeated by Treaty. It was defeated by Emperor Hirohito's surrender-treaty. Meaning, the United States had to maintain the Emperor of Japan as a kind of unifying figure at the head of the Japanese government in order to get the whole thing to surrender in an orderly fashion all at the same time and follow our orders (through him). As a matter of fact there were high-ranking Japanese military officers who were fully prepared and ready to defy Emperor Hirohito's surrender-order and take over portions of Japan and run different factions in endless guerrilla war against the foreign invaders if they could. With the ghost of Lieutenant Hiroo Onoda the Japanese could have persisted in guerrilla warfare against the Americans just like the Afghanis did, or North Vietnamese, maybe indefinitely. If it were not for the orderly surrender of Emperor Hirohito and his ministers Japan may well have become another 'Afghanistan' type situation. All of these political realities were known by military planners at the time. If the US had vaporized the Emperor himself, Japan would have descended into protracted guerrilla warfare of competing sub-groups, and sub-states, a type of uncontrollable 'Afghanistan' of many competing smaller tribes. So the Emperor was permitted to live and reign NOT out of American benevolence, but rather out of a political necessity. [**32C**]

Also, the space-invader Orion Group is balanced politically and militarily against the Galactic Federation of Worlds to whom they are opposed. [**27W**] [**A31**] Gross, overt, planet-busting or Nuking of our cities would almost certainly provoke an increased defensive Galactic-Federation response and intervention on earth and the solar-system. But if the Orions came to our leaders and hammered out a treaty, as they did with the MAJIC-12 military-government in 1954, they can hold up that treaty to the Galactic Federation of Worlds and say, in effect, *'see! They want us here. They agreed to it. You have no right by your own laws and ethics to deny the free-will choice of a developing people like the earthlings to interact with whomever they choose.'* And this puts the Galactic Federation and the Pleiadean peoples who care about us in somewhat of a moral dilemma. [**27W**] [**A31**]

For all of these reasons, which is the real political situation, Nuking or planet-busting of our major cities by The Orion Group or others, is almost politically impossible. The narrative that they must be non-aggressive or they would have bombed us back to the stone-ages already is way off the mark. Would you say that of the United States? We never Nuked Iraq or Afghanistan, after all. Would you call us then a peaceful people? The false-narrative of the Nuking back to Stone Age model masks the fact that there are many other ways to be aggressive and malevolent, and to try to take over the planet, which we will cover in subsequent chapters.

The Inter-Galactic Cold-War: Space-Elves vs. Bipedal Iguanas

*"Terrific. I'm about to get killed a million miles from nowhere . . .
with a gung-ho Iguana who tells me, 'relax.'"*
– Alex Rogan from the Last Starfighter, 1984

To understand the kind of clandestine competition that has been going on between the Galactic Federation of Worlds vs. The Orion Group here on Planet Earth I think it is helpful to draw an analogy from the past 100 years that a lot of people on earth understand already. From about 1945 to the Present-Day the United States and Russia have competed for influence around the globe. Both the CIA/DIA and the KGB/FSB have gone into many different developing countries around the world like Cuba, Venezuela, Columbia, Iraq, and Afghanistan to try to sway them to their cause. [33D] In the first two cases of Cuba and Venezuela the KGB was successful in winning those countries politically to the Russian side; in the case of Columbia the CIA was successful in winning the Columbian government to the USA side. Now, if the CIA or KGB does their job right nobody knows they have been there at all. This is for several reasons. First, the clandestine organizations don't want the opposing clandestine organizations to know what they are doing, when they are doing it, how they are doing it, where they are doing it, why they are doing it, or who they are doing it to. The CIA doesn't want the KGB to know what it is doing, and the KGB doesn't want the CIA to know what it is doing. Obviously this is an oversimplification of the process, and there are a lot of other different players involved as well, but I think it still facilitates understanding of the matter. The Spies are trying to get stuff done politically, yet while remaining hidden from the opposition AND the General Populations of all sides. The second reason is that the clandestine organizations don't want the native population of the given victim country to know what they are doing. It is possible that if the clandestine organization either CIA or KGB is too heavy-handed in the matter, the native population may get wise to it and resent the foreign meddling. It is possible for a nativist government to just kick out all the outsiders of whatever stripes like in Afghanistan, Iran, Vietnam, Somalia, or Israel for example. So for all these reasons the clandestine organizations, whether CIA/DIA or KGB/FSB try to remain politically invisible, and leave no fingerprints on their work if it can be avoided. [33D] In like manner The Orion Group and The Galactic Federation of Wolds have both sent in spies to compete over Earth, but are very careful to cover their tracks if at all possible. [A31] Sometimes they are unable to cover their tracks completely and then people see inexplicable weirdness.

Continuing the analogy, the CIA/DIA and KGB/FSB have a lot of tricky tools and methods up their sleeves to sway a given country to their cause. [33D] They can bribe politicians with gifts of money or advanced technology, in hopes of bringing them over to their side. They can fund the political parties they like. They can run propaganda AGAINST the political parties they don't like. They can fund politicians or candidates for President in a given country that most closely aligns with their ideals. They can organize demonstrations AGAINST candidates or politicians they don't like. They can even attempt to aid or foment Revolutions against governments and administrations they hate. As a recent example the CIA/DIA could have theoretically aided the demonstrators and Ukrainian Revolutionaries of the Euro-Maidan to victory over their Russian-leaning counterparts in 2013. In an extreme case a clandestine organization might assassinate a native President, Premier, or Prime-Minister who is oppositional to their cause in order to replace him or her with a candidate more favorable to their cause. Of recent memory the former President of Ukraine, Viktor Yanukovych, was widely known to be Russian-leaning, while the new President, Volodymyr Zelenskyy, was known to be NATO & US leaning. The Russians had meddled in Ukraine for decades in order to ensure the Presidents of Ukraine were favorable to their cause like Viktor Yanukovych. The CIA/DIA theoretically could have returned the favor by helping to back and install a Westward pro-NATO-leaning Ukrainian government after Euromaidan in 2014 with President Volodymyr Zelenskyy at its head. My goal here is not to take sides in this particular Slavic civil-war, but rather to illustrate the principal of how these power-politics work in real life.

Once we understand this "Cold-War" [33D] paradigm here on earth, man-vs.-man, it is much easier to understand how the Galactic Federation of Worlds and The Orion Group are competing for control of Planet Earth, with each side sending in spies to spy out the planet and manipulate key events, politics, and technology for the benefit of their respective factions. In this conceptual model neither side is omnipotent. The native population gets a say in the matter too. In the Earth-Historical examples of Afghanistan, Somalia, and Vietnam, the native population actually did expel all foreign empires both Russian-leaning and USA-leaning alike, and remained Independent, so that is a possible outcome as well.

The KGB/FSB and the CIA/DIA are in fact capable of wearing masks. Both metaphorically and actually. Since the 1960s high-quality full-latex head-masks with hair have existed for use by both sides. This is illustrated in any number of modern or Cold-War era Spy-films, but it is also a real-world reality and is one of the tools used by human clandestine organizations right here on earth. We can also imagine that an advanced civilization of Extraterrestrials would have even more elaborate, exotic, and effective means at their disposal for concealing the true identities of their operators.

In the case of the Pleiadean Extraterrestrials they don't need masks to be spies here on Earth. This is because the Pleiadean Extraterrestrials look sufficiently human to pass as human in just about any White-European society. [A31] Internally there are key genetic differences, for they live to about 700-years old. Their DNA is actually different at a microscopic level, seemingly superior to human DNA in certain ways, but outwardly they look to be basically Scandinavian with light-skin tone, light blond or brown hair, and mostly with blue or green eyes. When scouting out the Earth the Pleiadean spies need only don period-specific human clothes, learn English or another human language sufficiently to speak with an unidentifiable foreign accent, and then charm their way into the Pentagon or wherever else through ordinary job advertisements. In the past they have posed as Danish Doctors, European Nobility, and female secretaries looking for work in the US Pentagon, into which they were gladly accepted in a more paternalistic era with no problems.

In the case of Reptilian spies here on earth the job is a little bit more difficult because in their natural state they look like giant 6-foot tall talking Iguanas. Not exactly a physique apt to blend in to human societies. And they smell really bad, like sulfur, as if they just crawled up out of the pit of hell. [11K] Nevertheless, the Reptoids have a lot of sneaky spies crawling around all over the place by use of 3 primary methods:

Reptoid Spy Method #1: *Some but not all* Reptoids have a Species-specific ability to shapeshift for short periods of time. [3C] This is not a technological capability. It is a rare Species-specific ability of maybe only 1% of their population. It is more like how some humans are just born double-jointed, can do Parkour, or seduce women with ease. It seems to take a lot of mental-focus from them, however, and is not always 100% effective. I imagine it takes about the same level of mental-focus as for your dad with his dad-bod to walk around with his gut sucked in at a pool-party with a lot of hot women. One moment of inattention and the dad-bod gut pops back out again. Thus, many experiencers have reported seeing otherwise normal-looking people suddenly morph into having a Reptilian head. And that's why. Because it was a Reptilian-Spy. To not believe in or understand this is in my view an incredible level of ignorance. Like an Ostrich sticking his head in the sand with his butt hanging out for the whole universe to see. The Ostrich Theory won't save you. We must listen to the Old Elephant telling us about the ways of the Crocodile. About how he lurks just under the surface of the watering-hole. Try not to get eaten, my friend.

Reptoid Spy Method #2: The Reptoids have some advanced cloning sciences. This is a technological capability. In the past they have cloned a lot of blond-haired blue-eyed Pleiadean clones for this purpose. In addition to this they have consciousness-transfer science (soul-sucking) whereby they can place a Reptoid soul into a Pleiadean-clone body. This would have the added benefit of tainting their main opposition, the Pleiadean peoples and the Galactic Federation of Worlds with whatever crimes they were committing during the course of their normal duties. This is the more-advanced version of a Reptoid "Sheep-Dipped" Spy that they can now let loose on their enemies to undermine other civilizations. [A31]. So a lot of what you have been seeing on the news probably makes more sense now. The Reptoids would probably also have the ability to do this type of cloning with Earth-humans as well. This is a key understanding as this type of infiltration-takedown of various civilizations is the main Reptoid modus operani. [A31]

Reptoid Spy Method #3: The Reptoids also have whatever is akin to or an advanced version of the CIA/KGB latex-mask model. Essentially low-tech 'human suits'. I kid about the 'Henry-Kissinger-Suit' throughout this whole book as a kind of tong-in-cheek analogy for this concept. And as for the sulfur smell? Most of the time they just let it linger. Of course the Reptilians do not always wear masks or 'Henry Kissinger Suits' as they are uncomfortable and hot, and usually do not if they feel sufficiently secure within their joint underground Human-Alien bases. Thus, many human and military personnel have seen them in their full, demonic, bipedal-Iguana-form, stinking up the place to high heaven. [11K]

The long lifespans of almost 1,000 years for both of these opposing Alien groups makes it so they are quite content with long-range planning.

A centuries-long perspective for them is no problem. Many of their leaders may still be holding office, some centuries hence, when their plans come to fruition. But we Terrans have to get generational. For our part we have to do like I do: stand on the shoulders of giants, our forefathers, imbibing and culminating with their knowledge, then mentor up the next generations before we pass on. If we don't do that it is easier for us to get manipulated, as the Aliens sit back and bide their time, and hope the rest of the humans just forget about what RIGHTEOUS AEON and all the rest of our ancestors said.

The long-term Prospectus of The Orion Group is to take over the planet, slowly but surely, one politician at a time if necessary. Just like in the USA vs. Russia cold-war paradigm, **[33D] [3C]** the Aliens are playing the long-game, making key manipulations behind-the-scenes that they believe will lead the planet and its civilizations to their desired outcome. The Orion Group wants a tightly controlled humanity in a command-and-control Pyramidal Structure, in something like a 1984 Orwellian nightmare police-state, supposedly run by AI, but actually run by themselves. In tightly-compact ultra-high-density-cities. They do not want any free-range humans. They want brain-chip implantation of all earth's key leaders for total tracking and control. Once that is accomplished they would move on to the Police and Military. After that everyone else. A second line of effort is population-reduction until the world-population is at what they consider to be a more manageable size, of about five-hundred-million, to use as a kind of biological farm system. Killer-vaccines, Bio-weapons, and Genetically-engineered viruses are keys in their plans for reducing the world-population of earth. This plan is maybe only 30% complete. I do not believe that this series of nightmare-events will actually occur to completion. I'm just explaining what The Orion Group has been up to on the planet for the last 100 years and therefor why you see what you are seeing now. I believe this process will be arrested and reversed due to people like me and you and others that come after us. **[27Z]**

The long-term Prospectus of The Galactic Federation of Worlds for earth is that they want us to join their alliance. It is something like a cosmic NATO or a cosmic United Nations type situation. To be fair, they do try to give all types of different races and civilizations representation and something like an equal vote. So it is actually a type of Galactic-Republic, technically. **[A31] [12L]** (there you go all you Star-Wars nerds) Yet we must be careful here, too, because once you get jumped in, you're in, and probably can't get out. Earth would fall underneath the legal jurisprudence of The Prime Directive -their unified master code of laws, kind of like our US Constitution. To this end the Galactic Federation of Worlds people have a long-term strategy of buttering us up with bribes and sexy Pleiadean women in order to tempt us into joining. It's the *'catch more flies with honey'* strategy. For their part our large, industrious, war-like populations would be a nice addition to their alliance -maybe something like the US currently feels about India, or like the European Union feels about the United States. They have visions of arming up young, strapping, earth men-and-women (something like Starship Troopers), pointing us at their enemies, and saying in effect: 'go sick- 'em!' -And we would, because that's the way we are. Plus we have short lives anyway, so if we die in war at 20 or 40, . . . no great loss. Maybe kind of like how we might feel about hunting-dogs, police-dogs, or military-working dogs. It's our job to take that bullet (or laser-beam in this case).

By contrast, most of the Galactic Federation of Worlds peoples are Pacifist **[A31]**, decadent, addicted to pleasure, don't like war, don't like pain, lacking in discipline, sparsely populated, low birth-rate, because their men don't like to have sex and their women don't like to bear children, and it's all an egalitarian society so you can't make the women produce.

The Galactic-Federation-of-Worlds would want to create something like a 'French-Foreign-Legion' out of the Terrans, or a 'Terran-Foreign-Legion' in this case I guess, for the same reasons the French have a Foreign Legion -they don't really want to have to fight their own wars. And that's fine. There are millions of Terran-nutcases like myself that would join, and more being born every day -but we have to realize what we have, the 'human-capital' we have, and remember to leverage that at the negotiating table. From the Alien point of view we make good mercenaries and Soldiers as a Species, but we should exact from them a proper price for our services. -how about med-beds for Veterans for starters?

For all these reasons the Galactic Federation of Worlds wants Earth the Planet or the greatest coefficient thereof to join their military-alliance AGAINST their enemies, The Orion Group. Both of these Extraterrestrial factions are racing to try to control the development and destiny of mankind for their own ends. **[27W] [A31] [27Z] [20T] [8H] [3C] [30Z]**

The Galactic Federation of Worlds

". . . To boldly go where no man has gone before!"
– Captain Picard from Star-Trek the Next Generation opening
credits, 1987-1994

Much like Gene Roddenberry's 'Star Trek' there is a real Galactic Federation of Worlds. And indeed they go by a code of laws which they translate for us from an Alien language into English as: "The Prime Directive". A law which states that developing civilizations (like ours) are not to be messed with. One wonders how much was intentionally leaked to Screen-Writer Gene Roddenberry and his son over the years. **[27W]** **[A31] [26Z] [12L]**

This Federation of many different planets and species tries to get along by settling conflicts in a judicial manner guided by their unified code of law, translated into English as "The Prime Directive". To become a part of the Galactic Federation of Worlds, a whole planet or sentient species must meet a certain threshold of technological development, at least be space-faring, and the majority of its people or elected leadership agree to become a part of the mutual-defense treaty. In this way it is a kind of intergalactic-NATO or a kind of intergalactic-UN. **[27W] [A31] [26Z] [12L]**

And who might be the external threat to such an alliance? The Orion Group. Or as some may call it the Draco-Reptilian Empire. Many of the Planets, civilizations, and peoples now a part of the Galactic Federation of Worlds were victimized by The Orion Group in the past. **[27W]**

[A31] [26Z] [12L] In this analogy perhaps The Orion Group is somewhat like The Russian Federation. Earth the Planet is like Ukraine. And the Galactic Federation of Worlds is somewhat like NATO. I don't mean to be uncharitable to any of the human factions in this analogy, only to facilitate our understanding of the matter. Of course I believe we should be working with the actual human Russians in a united Earthling-Front to make sense of and deal effectively with the Extraterrestrial Threat to all of Planet Earth.

The religion (that they claim is not a religion) for most of the Galactic-Federation-of-Worlds Aliens is a type of New-Age-Pantheism where they believe a little bit of God is in all of us, and the planets and the stars and the fish and the birds and the clouds and the parameciums. In this respect it is Hindu-adjacent or Gia-adjacent in its philosophies. The Pleiadeans, foremost amongst the Galactic Federation in their contacts with Terrans, have many Earth-contacts amongst the New-Age Gurus and New-Age practitioners of Earth. **[27W] [A31] [26Z] [12L]** This also makes sense, as the first thing I would do in visiting a developing foreign-country would be to contact the local Christian pastor, who shares my faith and religion, and by extension probably most of my cosmology and politics. That is the family I would stay with in a developing foreign country and do business with. Those are the first people I would contact first in a foreign land. In like manner, the Pleiadeans, foremost among the Galactic Federation of Worlds (from our perspective) have tended to contact those New Age practitioners who most closely algin with their religion (that they claim is not a religion) and outlook on earth as a first step. Although the Pleiadeans do also contact and do business with a lot of high-ranking US Admirals and US Air-Force Generals who tend to be Evangelical-Christians of some stripes. So, perhaps some common cause can be made there as well.

Continuing in this vein it is interesting to note that the Galactic Federation of Worlds and The Pleiadeans are rabidly opposed to THE VACCINE **[A31]**, knowing it to be a technique of human population control instituted by The Orion Group and their human collaborators,

The Cabal/Deep-State/Shadow-Government/Control-Group. And so perhaps some common cause may be made between them and the Fundamentalist Jews, Christians, and Muslims on this planet such as myself.

The main problem that I foresee with The Galactic Federation of Worlds and the Pleiadeans foremost amongst them, is that they are just too damn nice. Too good-looking. Too beneficial. I foresee a situation worse than the Beatles Coming To America. It has already begun. Everyone will want to look like them, dress like them, play with crystals like them, get their technology, have sex with them. It will be insane. It will be like the fundamentalist Christian, Jewish, and Muslim parents trying to lock up their sons and daughters from the perversion of Elvis Presley and Rock-n-Roll to no avail. The more the Fundamentalists (such as myself) forbid, the greater the passion for the New Cool. The coolest of the Earthmen will have Pleiadean girlfriends. The New Age religion on Earth, now relatively small in number and only a fraction of the population, will be multiplied a thousand-fold due to the malevolent and irresistible influence of this seductive batch of Space-Invaders.

It must remain fore-most in our minds during this passage that the Earth rightfully belongs to the children of men, and Space-Invaders of whatever stripes do not belong here. The Pleiadeans and other Galactic Federation members will obey their own code of laws, The Prime Directive, if called out on the matter and forced to obey in a legal setting. Maybe somewhat like a developing country in Africa is able to go before the UN and demand that predatory US Companies or Churches withdraw from their native soil. The power of law is strong amongst the Galactic Federation of Worlds, and they go by it.

Pleiadeans

"Canst thou bind the sweet influences of Pleiades, or loose the bands of Orion?"

– Book of Job 38:31 KJV

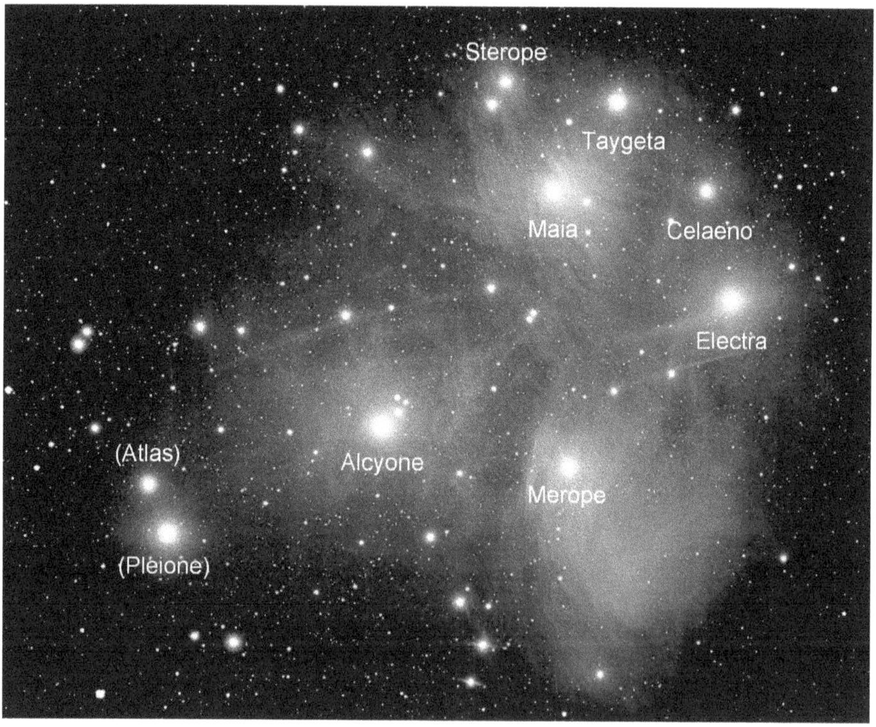

Pleiades Star Systems

The Pleiadeans are basically Space-Elves as a starting level of understanding. **[16P]** However, they have normal-looking ears. The pointy-ear thing must have been some type of legendary embellishment from someone who had a thing for pointy-ears. They generally come from the star-systems we classify as the Pleiades Star Systems. The Pleiadeans live for about 700 years which makes their societies more boring. **[27W] [A31] [26Z] [12L]** They have a very low birth-rate by comparison to humans because their men are super prudish and don't like to have sex, and it makes their women really frustrated. They will perhaps just have 1 child at 300 or 400 years old (corresponding roughly to our 30s or 40s I suppose). They view children as being precious and sacred, especially because of the effort their women have to go through in wooing their men. In a way the Pleiadeans are more sheltered as most pain, suffering, hunger, and want has been engineered out of their civilization. They call it a 'Post-Scarcity-Civilization' in contrast to our 'Scarcity-Civilization' where everyone goes around in the rat-race fighting over limited parking-spaces. By contrast the Earthlings are a type of 'Afghanistan' developing 3rd-world country. We are subject to a lot more pain, suffering, hardships, and lack than they due to our low level of technological development, and by having somewhat mean and ignorant societies. In the past some of the humans believed them to be immortal due to their (comparatively) long lifespans, but this was never true. Physiologically (and somewhat temperamentally) they resemble very closely to the Earthling Scandinavians. This is due to mixed bloodlines between them and us in that part of the world stretching back for thousands of years. **[16P]**

Approximately 3,000 years ago by my reckoning, the Pleiadeans had set up some terrestrial colonies in that part of the world, what we now call Northern Europe, to defend the developing bronze-age humans from Reptoid predation. Therefor they appear mythologically in human lore from that period as "Elves" or an "Eldar Race" in various now-dead Norse languages. **[16P]** The Reptoids appear in the legends as well, such as in the Legend of Beowulf. (Grendle is a hominid, two arms, two legs, but has scaled-skin, basically a bi-pedal Iguana Reptoid as I have been saying.)

From about 1,000 BC to about the time of Christ by my reckoning the Pleiadeans had permanent terrestrial enclaves in that part of the world for the purpose of aiding and protecting mankind primarily from Reptoid Predation. Only one problem. Some of their women-folk took a fancy to the strapping earth-men of the period, mostly the tribal warlords whom we nostalgically remember as princes and kings of the Irish, Saxons, Danes, and Getes. The Pleiadean women sometimes went native and intermarried with human bronze-age warlords. This gave rise to hybrid offspring and many of our most cherished legends from the period. ("Elven" princesses etc.) The legends regarding this Eldar people was passed down primarily through oral tradition in song throughout otherwise illiterate dark-age European tribes. (Illiterate meaning lacking a written language) And therefor such mythology suffered much embellishment, ascribing to the star-crossed foreigners Magical powers, the gift of immortality, and pointy ears, as examples of several misunderstandings. **[16P]**

This is perhaps a similar situation as to when in the modern, a young white English Nurse goes to some backwards African country governed by violent competing warlords. She goes there first-and-foremost out of love to minister to the precious little babies and pet their heads -orphans in that war-torn land, to feed them nourishing soup, and to guide them up in a better, more peaceful way. However, once she is there she starts to feel unexpected scary feelings for the best-looking, most-dynamic, most-ambitious, and most-violent of the local Warlords (or his son) with superior Stoiyl who she also can't help but see as the grown-up version of the precious baby boys for whom she is there to minister. Isn't her carnal attraction to him a part of her overall mission after all? And perhaps her love will tame his more murderous tendencies -a veritable triumph of love over hate, the most cherished dream of every woman in the universe. In comparison the other English doctors who surround her and don't protect her seem tame, weak, boring, and all too predictable -reeking of 'friend-zone' energy. That's basically what Pleiadean women think about their men. Thus she goes native and marries the local warlord, or his most violent son. This is basically what happened to the Vikings three-thousand years ago and how they got infiltrated by the Pleiadean Women:

Just as you can see in this recently re-created AI image out of our collective spiritual subconscious: the Pleiadean Princess is feigning weakness and using her advanced Alien mind-powers to enslave the strongest knight of the realm against the wishes of the other humans (who are throwing tomatoes at the illegal-Alien). This is because we still retain within us the distorted spiritual memories of our collective and legendary past:

Thus it became apparent to The Galactic Federation of Worlds that due to now intermingled blood-lines in that part of the Earth that the Pleiadeans were having far too great an impact on the civilization of man. They were therefor in breach of their own Prime Directive. Even though they had come to help, protect, and defend, they now found that the uncontrollable lust of their women for Anglo-Saxon German men was creating its own predicaments. Half-Breeds were living two and three-hundred years. (Tolkien's *Dunnedain,* which he intuited from the older Norse Legends) The General Population of humans was ever and rightfully distrustful of the manipulative 'Elven Princesses', -Pleiadean women playing princess in bronze-age mediaeval courts. Worst yet the human women were resentful of all their best men being snatched up by Foreigners. The 'Elven' harpies never seemed to die and would linger around generation after generation, manipulating as they went to the logic of some unintelligible cosmic force. Due to all these problems and the violation of the Prime Directive itself the kind of 'Elrond' councils of the day decided they all must leave the planet and allow the humans to develop their civilization on their own. Thus, the ancient Norse legends have a period of the Eldar peoples 'leaving', going away in 'ships' . . . across the sea or something. This was all understood through a Bronze-age lens and passed down through campfire songs and medieval bards so there is bound to be some embellishment. Now they are back in 2024. The Pleiadeans have returned to Earth. And all these same memes and predicaments shall be seen again to a greater and far worse extent. Because you thought you were progressing forward in time, but you are really just going around in circles.

The religion that they claim is not a religion:

According to the Pleiadean peoples and most of the Galactic Federation of Worlds peoples, all Sentient life are soul-fragments of the Supersoul, the Divine Source (and this is at least partially true) from somewhere exceeding the 9th dimension, a place of infinite love, peace, beauty, power and harmony. According to them therefore, God is in all of us, and all of us are partakers with God. They have different ways. Yet they ignore or omit (but not dare to deny) the Personhood and Sovereignty of God. This is the essence of Pantheism. According to the Pleiadeans as with other Spiritual New Agers: All souls are eternal and experience exact and perfect Karmic reward or punishment according to their behavior in following incarnations. At death souls ascend to the higher heavenly dimensions or fall down to the lower hellish dimensions based exactly and precisely upon what each one deserves or had earned. **[27W] [A31] [26Z] [12L]**

A kind of parallel exposition to the Christian Old-Covenant '*you reap what you sow*'. In comparing Pleiadean Cosmology to the Theologies of the Abrahamic Faiths I would contend that many of these precepts are the same in substance, only using differing terms, yet they ignore and omit (but not dare to deny) the personhood and Sovereignty of God, because they have a major beef with him.

Pleiadean Nuclear Arms Control Initiatives

*"Target distance three miles . . . Roger three miles . . . target in sight
. . . Where in hell is Major Kong?!*
Major Kong: "Ahhhhhhhhhhhh hhoooooooooooo! . . ."
[Rides the nuke to its target]
– Dr. Strangelove, 1964

When the nation of Pakistan developed the Atomic Bomb in 1984 it took the US State Department and Intelligence Community by surprise. [32B] There was probably a little cultural-bias here: I mean, Fundamentalist Arab Muslims aren't really that smart, right? Nevertheless, Pakistan *did* develop nuclear weapons with their own scientists, most of them last name Khan, (descended from Genghis Khan) and it was a big upset for the US intelligence community. A big problem. We immediately had visions of Pakistani clerics praising Allah as their ICBMs headed for the most densely populated cities of their arch-rival, India. We envisioned whatever the equivalent is of a Pakistani Mujahadin toting a nuclear suitcase bomb to the top of the Eiffel Tower and shouting Allah-Ahkbar! as he gleefully pushes the button in a nuclear-suicide attack. That's kind of how The Galactic Federation of Worlds feels about humans having Nukes. It is a Space-Age technology a thousand years ahead of our cultural, moral, ethical, and spiritual development to be able to handle. They make further claims that civilizations having gone down the Nuclear-tech-tree in the past tend to blow themselves up. This isn't their first rodeo says they. **[A31] [12L]**

Pleiadeans view Terrans with the Atomic bomb much as we here in the West might view 'The Islamic Bomb' of Iran or Pakistan. Basically as irresponsible violent societies that if allowed to develop too much military technology without the corresponding spiritual and ethical systems in place will go around Nuking everyone in the universe like the Nacht Waffen is doing right now. Thus, the Pleiadean line-of-effort #1 is to both nuclear-disarm the Terrans to an extent that we won't be dangerous in spaceships, while simultaneously trying to win us over to their side of the Galaxy as Super Soldiers to help them fight as front-line Shock-Troops against their arch-enemies, the Reptoids. Basically trying to re-direct our destructive energies against their enemies. You have to understand the real-politic here.

The dilemma the Pleiadeans are experiencing in this regard about the Terrans is kind of like if you have a young strong rambunctious Pit-Bull puppy that has already bitten several people; you can't decide whether to muzzle him, chain him, or maybe just pet him enough and rub his belly enough to make him really loyal to you and a really good guard-dog that will fight for you to the death in the future. Obviously they are not going to say these quiet parts out loud at the negotiating table, but that's basically what it is. They are metaphorically rubbing our belly.

Another way to view the deportment of the Pleiadeans and the Galactic Federation of Worlds towards the Earthlings might be similar to the way an 87-year-old-grandmother views a young gang of 13-year-old junior-high boys. Their natural inclination is to want to go outside into the neighborhood, find some sticks that can be fashioned into weapons, form a gang with hand-signs and tattoos, and then start beating each other with the sticks. As a matter of fact many groups of unsupervised young-men do form such types of gangs, and do naturally engage in street-to-street gang-warfare all the time all over the world even without having to be taught. Personally I view it as a type of Terran special ability. Your 87-year-old grandmother (and the Pleiadeans) already knows all this about 13-year-old boys and how they can be, and what mischief they can get into if left unsupervised. Therefor, as adults we strive to re-direct the natural impulses of such young-men into more productive channels by enrolling them in sports, band-camp, or yoga-class. That's kind of the way the Pleiadeans view most of the Earthlings.

Weirdly, we do not yet have any hard evidence that any of the other Extraterrestrial Groups possess nuclear weapons. Laser Beams? yes. Inter-galactic Starships? yes. Forcefields? yes. Zero-Point-Energy? yes. Clones of Hillary-Clinton? yes. Nanites? yes. Nukes? . . . We're not yet sure. It may be that the Atomic Bomb is a technology a thousand years ahead of its time; like it doesn't really belong in the diesel-punk era that the rest of humanity is currently in. Or it may be that their Tech-trees had developed in a different way using the power of crystals. Or that they chose not to pursue Atomic Bomb technology viewing it to be barbaric, redundant, or perhaps even out-of-date. Maybe somewhat the way we would view the ancient Chinese military doctrine of setting fires intentionally to burn an adversary's city to the ground or the medieval practice of lobbing dead cows over an enemy's castle walls. It appears there are several optional Tech-trees. the Galactic Federation has gone down a Tech-tree that relates to the power of crystals and energy frequencies. There is also a Nuclear tech-tree. The Pleiadeans claim that civilizations that have gone down the Nuclear Tech-tree in the past tend to blow themselves up, . . . but what do they know? We're special.

Due to their behavior and rhetoric on the matter, I would intuit that Nuclear Weapons belong to a special class of banned 'Weapons of Mass Destruction' that are patently both illegal and taboo in Galactic-Federation society. We can understand how an advanced civilization might develop this point of view. In the past their bold and absolutist demands of Terran Nuclear-disarmament would lead one to believe that the ban and taboo on these weapons is already a well-established precept and first-principal within their societies for thousands of years. Kind of like how Christian missionaries would have the gall to demand an immediate and absolute ban on cannibalism to a more traditional society. Nevertheless, Terrans do possess Nukes, and the Aliens are really worried about it. **[A31] [12L]**

In terms of Terrans possessing nuclear weapons, this is a big no-no for the Pleiadeans and Galactic Federation of Worlds Aliens. A big no-no that has already happened. A big no-no that seemingly can't be undone. A big no-no that they don't know what to do about. Terrans via the Nacht Waffen are already causing massive problems for the Pleiadeans and the rest of the Galactic Federation of Worlds throughout the Galaxy. [A31] As discussed before, the Reptoids already developed several generations of German people into Super-Solders to fight on behalf of their space-empire, The Orion Group. Germans which today we call The Natch Waffen / or in English: "The Dark Fleet" space-NAZIs blood-line descended from the Waffen-SS (wounded-Waffen) empowered by Reptoid spaceships and technology. [4D] [8H] [30Z] [3C] [37H] The Reptoids breed German Super-Soldiers like hunting-dogs. Do you see how cunning the Reptoids are? They have German people to do their dirty-work for them. The Reptoids have unleashed this German Super-Soldier group on the rest of the cosmos, and the Space-NAZIs who are our first human emissaries to other civilizations, are currently going around to the most peaceful of the other planets in the Galaxy and hitting them with Nukes. This has forced the Pleiadeans and the rest of the Galactic Federation of Worlds to ask the question: What about when the Americans become spacefaring? Are they going to start hitting us with Nukes? What about when the Russians become space-faring, are they going to start hitting us with Nukes? What about when the Chinese become spacefaring? Are they going to start hitting us with Nukes? What about when the Hawaiians become space-faring? Are they going to start hitting us with Nukes? I can only speak for the Americans, and I can assure you guys that when we become Spacefaring we will most likely not hit you with Nukes, unless we decide we don't like you. The Pleiadeans and the rest of the Galactic Federation of Worlds Aliens view the militancy of the Earthlings, such as myself, maybe somewhat like we here in the West might view a nuclear-armed Pakistan. It's a fact. It's a problem. It's only a matter of time before things get really interesting.

In response to the hyper-militancy of the Earthlings such as yours-truly, the Pleiadeans and the Galactic Federation of Worlds seem to have come up with a very wise, long-term, well-thought-out, multi-pronged, integrated, foreign-policy towards us that has at least six major prongs, or Lines-of-Effort (and I would expect nothing less from Space-Elves):

1. Disarm.
2. Pacify.
3. Ingratiate.
4. Litigate.
5. Ally with.
6. Intermarry.

Disarm. In the first prong, or Line-of-Effort of the Pleiadean and Galactic Federation of Worlds foreign-policy towards Earth, they are trying to talk us down, talk us out of our Nukes. This was the very first item they put on the table in negotiating with President Eisenhower in 1954 [A31], so we know it is important to them. [12L] Kind of like how NATO talked the Ukrainians into nuclear-disarmament with assurances of military protection if Russia ever threatened to invade. Plus they make the case that Nukes are mean and barbaric, beneath the standards of an ethical civilization. We've already suffered through hours of these types of moralistic lectures that make your mom's or dad's moralizing lectures about responsibility look tame. They are willing to offer bribes of advanced (peaceful) technology and monetary incentives both to governments and to individuals to do so. Probably much of the Nuclear-non-proliferation efforts around the globe over the last century were sponsored by, or at least significantly aided and abetted by Pleiadean agents and agents of the Galactic Federation of Worlds. [A31] [12L] It just has their type of spiritual and moralizing rhetoric written all over it.

This line-of-effort is probably not going to work. Nuclear arms have already proliferated too greatly around the planet and in space amongst many of the various human tribes and groups to include corporate entities, The Nacht Waffen, the US, Russia, China, Pakistan, Iran, North Korea, The US Marine Corps, Kim-Jug-Un and Donald Trump. How the hell are you going to disarm all that at the same time? Or even piece-meal? So that line-of-effort is probably going to fail. The better angels of mankind are probably not going to prevail in this sphere of thought, or Line-of-Effort. I don't foresee all or any of those groups willingly giving up their Nukes any time soon. The Pleiadeans have to know this, right? It would be like trying to get a Tripple-A baseball player to give up his favorite lucky baseball-bat. Like asking Thor to give up his hammer (he loves his hammer). It's just not going to happen. What is even the point of asking nicely if you know that asking nicely isn't going to work? Either you're too obtuse to realize that Thor loves his hammer, or you're asking nicely just for the purpose of trying to show the Galaxy that at one point in Time you tried to ask nicely first. Which leads me to my next point.

What about beaming down strategically to all the known-points on Earth they know nuclear-weapons are stored and either deactivating or confiscating them? I mean, they do have something like a star-trek tele-porter to do so. And they've been mapping out our nuclear arms sites for decades. [22V] [21U] We've detected Pleiadean and Armani Tau Cetians UFO scout-craft zipping, hovering, and orbiting around our nuclear sites for decades now, [22V] [21U] even shot some of them down and probed the captured pilots. And for all my razzing them about Pleiadean wuss-iness, they do have some enterprising and smart Astronauts similar to Picard, Riker, Jordi, Warf, and Dr. Beverly Crusher from Star-Trek The Next Generation capable of making a strategic and daring raid like that; a simultaneous operation to beam-down and disarm or confiscate our Nukes that they would assuredly believe to be in all of our best-interests. So I would be wary of some type of large-scale nuclear-deactivation or confiscation raid from them in the future like that. They say that past behavior is the best indicator of future performance. Well, the Pleiadeans and Tau Cetians of The Galactic Federation of Worlds actually have elec-tronically-deactivated some of our American Nukes in the past at dif-ferent bases in North and South Dekota for a short limited time, [22V] [21U] through what we would now call electronic-warfare (although it was unknown at the time). There have been different reports of these types of electronic-warfare attacks on our nuclear arsenals from the Pleiadeans and Tau Ceti of The Galactic Federation of Worlds stretching back for decades. [22V] [21U] But they probably haven't had the logistics fully in-place to deactivate all the Nukes around the world simultaneously or permanently in the past as we keep some in silos, some on planes, some on submarines, and some in your dad's briefcase. I would advise our military forces, and especially our nuclear arms security teams to remain vigilant, and to be on the lookout for any sexy Pleiadean women in tight-fitting spacesuits trying to talk us out of our Nukes.

Pacify. In their pacification Line-of-Effort, the Pleiadeans and Galactic Federation of Worlds people seek to make the human character, psyche, and spirit more peaceful in nature, and less militant. I supposed in a political-science sense we would probably term these types of efforts 'influence operations' or 'Psychological Operations'. This includes hosting New-Age Yoga and meditation seminars. It includes types of wide-scale psionic bombardment of earth that effects people's dreams, with messaging regarding reincarnation, Karma, essentially their Pantheistic religion-type, such as the wide-scale psionic messaging program throughout the 1990s and early 2000s that resulted in the film 'Cloud Atlas' (Oh yes! we know about that one too!) But the film was a flop at the box-office and featured Tom Hanks who has now fallen out of favor, so this line of effort doesn't seem to be going very well either. One wonders how much of a hand they may have had in the peace-and-love hippie and New Age movements of the 1970s. This is about character and personality modification on a civilizational-scale that they hope will eventually result in policy changes they deem beneficial over time, such as less war, less militancy, less focus on turning every piece of technology into weapons etc.. [A31] [12L] Pacification efforts that we should resist with all the energy of a rabid chinchilla.

Ingratiate. In their Ingratiate Line-of-Effort the Pleiadeans and Galactic Federation of Worlds people want the Earthlings to be happy with them.

They are not trying to sow bad blood like the Reptoids by abducting everyone and committing crimes against humanity. The Pleiadeans and Galactic Federation of Worlds people view negative activities like these to be counter-productive, because they believe in Karma religiously, and because they know that even humans have historical-memory and are prone to blood-feuds if we feel we have been wronged. Thus, the Pleiadeans and Galactic Federation of Worlds people are trying to sow good-vibes at all costs amongst the Earthlings, which they believe will reap them a Karmic reward in the future, and better political relations with humanity overall going forward. [A31]

To be fair, the Pleiadeans and Galactic Federation of Worlds people have sown this planet and solar-system with wise debts of gratitude that will be hard for us to shake free of. -Kind of like when your parents paid for your expensive fancy college education and now you're never going to hear the end of it for the rest of your whole life. Pleiadean commanders Val-Thor and Thor-Han-Erydion have performed multiple Orion-Group abduction rescues of Terrans and Terran children for decades now. [A31] With their ships they have performed interstellar interdiction of enemy Orion-Group slaver ships that were either taking or seeking to abduct Terrans from Earth. Maybe somewhat like the British Navy was used in the 1800s to interdict slave-ships from Africa bound for the Americas. [34E] I hate to admit it, but this is much genuine good-will sown towards us that will be hard for Christian Fundamentalists such as myself to fully poison. It will also set up mankind to be much more inclined towards actually joining the Galactic Federation of Worlds military-alliance in the future, which is their next Line-of-Effort. [A31] [12L]

Litigate. In their long-term-plan the Pleiadeans and Galactic Federation of Worlds people want Earth the Planet, or the greatest coefficient thereof to sign-on to their Galactic Federation of Worlds military-alliance and to the Prime Directive code of law, kind of like a big galactic constitution. [12L] [27W] [A31] [26Z] [8H] We have to be wary here, because just as the Confederate States of America found out once upon a time, once you sign-on to such a constitution, you may not ever be able to withdraw. Just as we saw during The War of Northern Aggression here in the United States in the 1800s. This would bring Earth the Planet, and potentially every human being thereof, underneath the Prime Directive Code of Laws crafted long ago by a confederation outer-space Aliens. It would give the Galactic Federation of Worlds a lot more control of Earth and peace-of-mind if we were to fall withing the framework of their legal-system, The Prime Directive. If we were to accept that as a First Principal. It would make us as a people and a planet a lot more manageable in their view. **[12L] [27W] [A31] [26Z] [8H]** That's not good. The decision-point here is something like European nations deciding if they want to be a part of NATO, or the European Union or not.

It won't be long until the Pleiadeans and Galactic Federation of Worlds start to nag us about reading though The Prime Directive and voting on it in to adoption as a legal framework. They are already starting to nag a little bit now. And the nagging will only intensify over time. First of all the Prime Directive is really boring, kind of like a Death-by-Power-Point type situation. Second of all it's too long and complicated. Third, once you're in, you're in. It's like the American Sates that came together to fight against Great Brittain during the Revolutionary War but then couldn't back out later during the War of Northern Aggression. In a few hundred years we might suffer a Federation invasion if we try to back out. And lastly, and most importantly, we already have our own laws. Despise the Free-Lunch I say; to hell with The Prime Directive! As Jews, Christians, and Muslims, we have our own code of laws as derivatives of God's Cosmic Law and that's good enough for me.

Ally with. *'our Germans are better than their Germans'.* If all else fails the Pleiadeans and Galactic Federation of Worlds people at least want the rest of the Earthling commandos on their side when we take to the stars. If all else fails they at least want a military-alliance with the rest of the Earthlings of Earth, minus The Nacht Waffen, **[12L] [27W] [A31] [26Z] [8H]** -so that we can play the role of front-line Shock-Troops against The

Orion Group and their Human-German-Super-Soldiers that are already The Orion Group's front-line Shock-Troops arrayed against them. **[8H] [4D] [3C] [30Z] [27W] [A31] [26Z] [12L]** So they can say like in the film *The Right Stuff, 1983* - *'our Germans are better than their Germans'.*

Essentially we have the manpower they have the technology. Pleiadean worlds are sparsely populated by comparison. **[A31]** The earth as a kind of 'Pandora' jungle-world is densely populated by comparison (the Aliens claim over-populated, but they are wrong). Our people have fast learning-curves, baby-booms, fast-maturation, and short lifespans. We have millions of violent young men that would jump at the chance to be rolled into some type of 'Star-Ship-Troopers' Regiments to aid the Pleiadeans in their war-efforts against the Reptoids. But we also have to realize what we have, the value we bring to the negotiating table and not give away the planet in bad-deals to outer-space aliens of whatever stripes. We have the Infantry they have the Space-Force is another way of looking at it. Yet, our people have, do, and will also make excellent Star-Fighter pilots (this is not always the case with every Species, such as the Greys who drive like Asians and often crash). The added benefit being that there are a lot more of us Terrans to train up as potential star-fighter-pilots than Pleiadeans, and we don't mind going out in a blaze of glory at a young age. In this paradigm you can kind of view Pleiadeans like French people -beautiful, refined, snooty, pacifist, well-educated, take long vacations, kind of wussi, don't like war, don't want to fight their own wars, trying to live long cushi lives eating tasty food, of an ancient civilization that still needs a lot of help in the modern by Americans to survive. And by contrast the Terrans are more like Americans: gunslingers by birth, rugged individualists, primitive survivalists, over-sexed.

Personally I think it's fine to ally with The Pleiadeans or The Galactic Federation of Worlds as a military expedient for a short and limited time if necessary, for a fixed period, to keep them on their toes. As long as we exact a heavy price out of them for our services. It's kind of like when you get married and your wife just sits around all day on the couch watching day-time soaps eating potatoes-chips getting fatter and fatter demanding more and more food like the plant from *'Little Shop of Horrors',* -there's no accountability. But if you keep her as your girlfriend that can be jettisoned and kicked to the curb at any moment, she has to remain lean and slender and keep giving you nice back-massages to keep you coming back for more. So Ally-with, but don't marry the Galactic Federation of Worlds, I say.

Better yet, put their whole legal-system in a bind and legal conundrum by agreeing to ally with the Pleiadean nation ONLY for a short and limited time, or for a specific purpose, but NOT the entire Galactic Federation of Worlds Republic as a whole. This will put the councils of the Federation into some kind of nightmare-conundrum, diplomatic tailspin because individual alliances of individual worlds or Nations within the Galactic Federation as component parts with an external force is probably off-limits within the rules of their republic, or must at least require special permission from its masters. If done correctly it will have the added benefit of driving a long-term wedge between the Galactic Federation of Worlds and the Pleiadeans, and moving the Pleiadean nation further into OUR camp and not vis-a-versa as a third force. The long-term goal here is the Triumph of the Abrahamic Religions over the Pleiadean peoples to effectuate their reconciliation with the Cosmic-Creator, God; and has the potential to wrench them politically out of the grasp of the Pantheist Galactic Federation of Worlds and all their freaks. It will force the Pleiadean nation to choose a side and has the potential to rip the Galactic Federation of Worlds in two as an added benefit. < This is the diplomatic move they never saw coming, and has the potential to amplify Terran diplomatic leverage a thousand-fold as an emergent force over the next 400 years. Thus, rather than diplomatically conquering planet Earth as they intend through negotiation, a steady-stream of Pleiadeans and probably even Armani-Tau-Cetians would gradually start to defect to us instead -kind of like all the different people from around the world who defected to America over the last 200 years. This underhanded diplomatic strategy would really have the ability to kick the Galactic Federation of Worlds in their metaphorical balls for hundreds of years to come, and de-rail most of their carefully-laid plans.

I think in the overall galactic scheme of things, the Galactic Federation of Worlds probably needs us more than we need them. Therefor there's no need to subject ourselves to their Prime Directive Legal Framework. Kind of like how the Europeans need the Americans a lot more than the Americans need the Europeans in the diplomatic context of NATO, or whenever a war starts. Kind of like the French . . . always there when they need us. The right policy here, I believe, is to make fixed-term military-alliances with the Galactic Federation of Worlds in say, 5-year increments. This will give us Earthlings a lot more leverage over the relationship, and once they start pushing their global New-Age religion over Earth too much we can break it off and go full TERRA IMPERIUM MAGNUS to punish them.

Intermarry. In the final result the Pleiadeans are sure to resort to sex in an attempt to control the destiny of the human race, **[A32] [A33] [36G]** just like they did away back in the dark ages. **[16P]** The Donald Trumps, Putins, and Elon Musks of the future will all have Pleiadean wives, and half-breed Pleiadean children. If I become a major public figure, I too will probably have a Pleiadean wife and Pleiadean children. This will probably be the most effective mechanism of control whereby they will be able to influence Terran governmental policy at a very high level and on a long-term bases in order to bend it towards their manipulative ends for thousands of years.

The Armani-Tau-Cetians Are Too Cool for School

Somewhat like the Italian Carabinieri, the human-looking Armani Tau Cetians are an athletic Outer-Space-Alien Species that are a part of The Galactic Federation of Worlds. (Not to be confused with the non-human Tau-Cetians that look like Pepe-the-Frog) Other than looking like Italian surfers in wetsuits the Armani Tau Cetians are basically human-looking in appearance. They will probably be somewhat miffed for me saying this, but this race has been given the hard job of disarming all of Planet

Earth's Nukes by force if necessary. And by force they mean disarm or confiscate all our Nukes completely from every country on Earth all at the same time without incurring a single human casualty. This last part is key because Stalin said, and it remains true: *'A single death is a tragedy, a million, a statistic.'* The Armani Tau Ceti and the Galactic Federation of Worlds don't want that single human casualty to become a sore-spot, like Ashley Babbit, in centuries to come. They don't want us to have the history of the one brave United States or Russian military officer that held on to his briefcase-Nuke and got vaporized while doing his duty holding on to that Nuke. They don't want to see his face again and again every fleet week and 4th of July or May-Day parade every year for the next three centuries. They don't want it to become a sore-spot between Terran and Galactic-Federation-of-Worlds relations. Because in the long-run they want to make friends. But they don't want us to have Nukes. Do you see the problem? Because they do. It's kind of like your hipster-girlfriend in college can't stand your exotic gun-collection from around the world, but still wants to get married in the long-run. She has to try to convince you to get rid of it on your own accord, or make up some excuse about how it all got stolen one unfortunate night by her friend in the Italian mafia, and then apologize for it afterwards. That's basically what the Armani Tau Cetians and Galactic Federation of Worlds people are trying to do. The Galactic Federation has been trying to talk us down and out of our Nukes for almost a century now starting with President Eisenhower in 1954. [15O] [23W] But if that polite strategy doesn't work, if the nagging doesn't work, the Galactic Federation will have assigned the Armani Tau Cetians people and/or Ashtar Command to be the fall guys and gals, the 'bad-cops' so-to-speak, the 'Italian-mafia-friend' by way of analogy who will accidentally come by one night and make off with all of your Nukes. Then the Pleiadeans and Galactic Federation of Worlds people will play the 'good-cops' and will apologize for how the Armani Tau Cetians/and or Ashtar Command acted, how they 'got out of hand' and here is all this great other peaceful technology to make up for it, and why don't you all just forget about the Nukes anyway?

For one, the Armani Tau Cetians have been caught and shot-down multiple times snooping around our Nuclear Silos. **[22V] [21U]** And whenever we try to proliferate our Nukes to a new country, there are Armani Tau-Cetian UFOs buzzing around our aircraft like with Malaysia Airlines Flight 370. And then whenever we shoot down one of their UFOs snooping around one of our Nuclear-Silos and waterboard the pilots we get nothing but name, rank, and serial-number. Like, MI Captain: 'what were you doing snooping around our Nuclear Silos in South Dekota, it's cold up here and boring and the women are ugly.' *silence* MI Captain: 'What was your mission?' *silence*. So there is a blank spot as to what the Armani Tau-Cetians are doing snooping around our Nukes that they do not want us to know what they are doing. Suspicious? I think so. Also, Several times Armani Tau Cetians UFOs have shot Directed Energy Weapons at both dummy nuclear warheads, and real nuclear warheads in-flight, **[22V] [21U]** probably thinking a part of our military chain-of-command like Airforce General Curtis LeMay had finally gone crackers and pushed the button for reals.

The Armani Tau-Cetians as a race and/or Ashtar Command mercenary group as an organization have been appointed the politically-necessary role of being the 'bad-cops' to stop our Nukes. Conversely the Pleiadeans are to play the 'good-cops' the nice guys, the negotiators. Who will then apologize for the Armani Tau Cetians and/or Ashtar Command mis-deeds afterwards if necessary. The two Species and/or organizations are distinct enough so as to be separate in the Terran mind so that one can take the fall as a Scapegoat, and exonerate the other, but all of them are human-looking enough to snoop around here at our college-parties as long as they wear Levis and Ray-Bans. It is a very sophisticated strategy being employed by the Galactic Federation of Worlds. It's also a case of the white-skinned Aliens (Errahel Pleiadeans) tasking the brown-skinned Aliens (Armani Tau-Cetians) to do their dirty-work for them. Kind of like how Northern Italians look down upon Southern Italians. This has all been carefully coordinated secretly and at the top-levels of The Galactic Federation of Worlds government that we penetrated with Miss-Universe beauty-pageant winners. This isn't their first rodeo, after all. But it's not my first rodeo either. They have had a lot of practice at this type of thing for thousands of years. The only monkey-wrench in it is if we realize how manipulative they can be, like your mom.

Men of Earth in Grave Danger

"LANCELOT: Yes, you were. You were in terrible peril.
GALAHAD: Look, let me go back in there and face the peril.
LANCELOT: No, it's too perilous.
GALAHAD: Look, it's my duty as a knight to sample as much peril
as I can.
LANCELOT: No, we've got to find the Holy Grail. Come on!"
– Monty Python and The Holy Grail, 1975

If we are going to address the Alien problem we must address first and foremost the greatest menace to the peace of the Galaxy: Pleiadian Women. A horrifying truth has emerged, and is emerging from around the globe. As Intelligence Analysts we look for trends. Not hearsay, not the one-off, but persistent, unignorable patterns of abuse from around the world over time. In sifting through and amalgamating all the data a disturbing trend presents itself stretching back decades. [36G] [A32] [A33] Men from around the world who do not know each-other, from different countries, different continents even, in different years and decades, have reluctantly and shamefacedly divulged a shockingly similar tale to the authorities. With horror, we the Intelligence Analysts are compelled to follow where the data leads. The standard tale goes something like this: A single middle-aged man of German descent is sleeping at home, at night, all doors and windows locked. His domicile is sufficiently removed from neighbors so he is unable to call for help. He is awakened somewhere around midnight or shortly thereafter in the small-hours to find 1, 2, or even 3 Pleiadian Women in his room, appearing to be perhaps in their early 20s, Swedish or Scandinavian-looking with blond or platinum-white hair and blue or green eyes, indistinguishable from other earth-women except for their unnaturally idealized figures. But make no mistake these Pleiadean females are in reality and in most cases hundreds of years old and they prey upon much younger earth-men as a way of life. This Pleiadian female or females then overpowers the middle-aged German man with the use of advanced Alien mind-powers and performs unspeakable, shameful acts upon him, like the daughters of Lot, which he is powerless to resist. These horrendous ordeals have sometimes lasted for hours. **[36G] [A32] [A33]** This is an area where we need to trust men. We estimate that for every one of these ordeals that gets reported to the authorities, at least ten more go un-reported, the victims being too traumatized even to seek help for their irreparable psychological damage, a form of PTSD. To make matters worse many hybridized children have now been born of the Pleiadean Women due to these unions. Children of mixed Pleiadean and Terran blood playing with crystals abord the Starship Excelsior whom the Pleiadean Women cherish and teach Calculous at a young age as a kind of sick trophy for their misdeeds. **[A32] [A33] [36G]**

We have included an image below that most of the victims agree roughly approximates the cosmic intruders:

One can only imagine the horror experienced by the men who have been so victimized. Earth men of Germanic descent are at particular risk of being targeted, and have been targeted for this kind of grotesque abuse in Australia [36G], Canada, Germany, Austria, France, Great-Britton, and the United States. [A32] [A33] [36G] As you can see it is a grave and ongoing crime against mankind of cosmic proportions as the earth-men are unable to resist the powerful Alien mind-control of the Pleiadian Women. Carried to its logical conclusion, the uncontrollable rapine of the Pleiadean Women upon man may one day dilute the pure Adamic DNA of humanity to the point of non-existence, even putting the true and orig-inal human race on the brink of extinction. [A32] [A33] [36G] [28X]

Any future negotiations with the Pleiadeans must address this met-aphorical 800-pound Pleiadian Woman in the room as a central issue. Their victims should be paid Reparations. If hybrid children were cre-ated from such unions (which we know there have been) Alimony should be paid to the men who were victims of these abuses by the Pleiadean women, along with the establishment of lawful visitation rights to the Earthmen's biological children in order to ensure such children do not fall to the Pantheistic woke brainwashing of their corrupted New Age moth-ers. Also, joint-custody of such children with equal-time visitation and custody rights must be adjudicated between two such parents and the two civilizations. The Pleiadeans will/shall/must respect this as the power of both law and the spirit of equality is strong amongst them. We must also consider that since these children of the joint unions have been in custody of their Pleiadean mothers for many years and decades in some case -the dads deserve at least as much time retroactively. This is a matter of Earth-men's rights. This will have the added benefit of instilling in such children Christianity in some cases, as some of the dads are nominally Christian, which will then begin to take over the rest of their civilization like it did the Roman Empire, as a generational, long-term process. (Meeting our strategic long-term goals for the conquest of the Galaxy in the name of Jesus Christ.) Apologies (at a minimum) should be issued to the Earth-men by the Pleiadean Women themselves, individually, in-person, and not as a group or political apology only. The Pleiadean women should then be forced to apologize in-person to their victims and bring snacks (as a goodwill offering). Then, according to Jewish, Christian, and Islamic law she must adopt the religion of her chosen husband with whom she already has children, and faithfully serve him, making dinner, washing dishes, doing laundry, and not talking back for howeversolong he should live. (which from her perspective shouldn't be too long)

This truth-and-reconciliation effort should not be nearly so difficult as it first may seem. First of all, the Pleiadeans themselves keep excellent records, by virtue of their advanced technology **[A31] [12L] [27W]**; and we, the Terrans keep excellent records also by virtue of our Matrix-Like 1984-esque malevolent world-wide Big-Brother Police-State, created mainly by the United States. **[19S]** Thus, reconstructing the truth of these crimes on either the victim's or perpetrator's side should not be hard at all. All that must be done is that the ranking representatives of the Pleiadean Command should meet with the ranking representatives of our Military-Intelligence apparatuses and the two compare notes as to what really happened. Our Military-Intelligence apparatus is able to vet and verify all the Terran victims, and the Pleiadean Command should be able to sus out all the perpetrators: something like examining Scotty's transporter logs to see which Pleiadean Women snuck out in the dead of night on a raid without informing her superiors. For make no mistake, these Florence-Nightengale forays by the Pleiadean Women are violations of their own code of laws, ethics, and policies as well on the Galactic Federation side. And especially the part of The Prime Directive that preludes significant interference with Developing Civilizations such as our own. **[12L]** Surely widespread rapine of a planet's middle-aged German men qualifies in this category. The worst crime is that I myself have not yet been personally targeted.

Vichy USA & The Human Collaborators

FORBES BUSINESS AEROSPACE & DEFENSE Jan 13, 2014,11:08pm EST

by Contributor Michael Peck

"Documents leaked by NSA whistleblower Edward Snowden conclusively prove that the United States has been ruled by a race of tall, white space aliens who also assisted the rise of Nazi Germany in the 1930s.

. . .

Snowden, who has been given asylum in Russia, leaked documents that a race of extraterestrial "tall whites" arrived on Earth, helped Nazi Germany build a fleet of advanced submarines in the 1930s, and then met in 1954 with President Dwight Eisenhower "where the 'secret regime' currently ruling over America was established."

. . .

"Most disturbingly, this [Russian] FSB report warns, is that the 'Tall White' agenda being implemented by the 'secret regime' ruling the United States calls for the creation of a global electronic surveillance system meant to hide all true information about their presence here on earth as they enter into what one of Snowden's documents calls the 'final phase' of their end plan for total assimilation and world rule."

. . .

Meanwhile, the U.S. government is embroiled in a "cataclysmic" power struggle between President Obama, who heads the alien shadow government, and some unknown force [Q] that opposed the U.S.-alien alliance. "Most to be feared by Russian policy makers and authorities, this [FSB] report concludes, is if those opposing the 'Tall White' 'secret regime' ruled over by Obama have themselves aligned with another alien-extraterrestrial power themselves. [the Galactic Federation of Worlds]"

. . . Forbes contributor Michale Peck ridicules the FSB report leaked by Snowden as Russian propaganda in this 2014 article, but I give the [Russian] FSB props for summing up the real situation as succinctly as possible. [37H]

The Alien menace became more apparent in 1947 due to the Roswell, New Mexico UFO crash. [9I] In response to this exotic and unknown threat from the stars, and in a state of fear, the Truman Administration issued certain secret Executive Orders that placed the strategic military footing of the United States regarding Aliens firmly within the hands of a council of 12 picked men, top-ranking Generals and Scientists. [A31] This was probably done from a pragmatic security standpoint to take pressure off of the person of the President himself with the idea that the President as one man was too vulnerable to Alien mind-control or death-ray vaporization at any given moment from the cosmic intruders. At least a council of 12 men, dispersed across the world in underground bases would be harder to target all simultaneously, even by Aliens, and even if a portion thereof were assassinated or mind-controlled, the remainder would be able to direct the military-government of the United States into some kind of retaliatory response. They probably thought this arrangement was the best mitigation of the Alien threat they could do at the time given our comparatively inferior technology and Alien control of the skies and space. Thus the overall strategic military footing of the United States regarding Aliens was actually ceded to the MAJIC-12 group in 1947. **[15O] [A31]** The idea was that the President was cut out of the loop for his own benefit and safety. It would be useless for the Aliens to put pressure on the President henceforth because the real military decisions regarding the Alien problem were being handled by the MAJIC-12 council. In a similar state-of-mind MAJIC-12 would make a series of agreements with the Greys and The Orion Group in 1954 behind the back of President Eisenhower, **[A31]** that they probably thought gave the US and the Earthlings the best chance to learn and develop the Alien's military technology while stalling an outright 'Independence-Day' style invasion. I'm sure they thought themselves to be the saviors of the USA and the planet by brokering this agreement with the Aliens every bit as much as Marshal Philippe Pétain thought himself the savior of the French People by brokering an agreement with the Germans during World War 2 which we now refer to as 'Vichy France'.

Looking back we now view Vichy France in history as basically being synonymous with the NAZI state, as it essentially did their bidding in every practical way that mattered. But at the time Frenchmen living in the southern portion of 'unoccupied' France viewed Marshal Philippe Pétain and the Vichy Government as having saved their independent national sovereignty by brokering a skillful agreement with the Germans that at least saved them the specter of goose-stepping German formations in their streets (of Southern France) and spared them from direct home-invasion by the Gestapo (in Southern France). Instead, the French police themselves would serve the same role, and what remained of the French military would be used in the service of German goals without having to be directly commanded by German officers. It's kind of like in Casa Blanca where Loui as the French Chief-of-Police gets to think he's in charge and independent until Major Strasser shows up as an 'ally'. In this analogy just like French Police Captain Louis Renault in Casablanca, the MAJIC-12 military government isn't exactly thrilled to be underneath the thumb of Alien Foreign Powers, or beholden to them, but for whatever reason aren't quite ready to join the true 'Free French' resistance movement with Rick and me either. [Q]

Just like with the Vichy France situation, in reality the series of agreements that MAJIC-12 made with the Aliens just served to warp the entire military infrastructure of the United States toward the accomplishment of Alien goals. **[15O] [A31]** A lot of civilians would be involuntarily abducted in the dead of night by the Greys, as per the agreements, and medical experimentation performed. This was often accompanied by the harvesting of women's eggs **[Stolen Seed, Evil Harvest w/ Karin Wilkinson]** and/or advanced versions of 'Spin the Bottle' with other abducted Terrans of the opposite sex, and the subsequent creation of Grey-human hybrids. Sometimes the MAJIC-12 military-industrial complex would then abduct the same persons again afterwards, just to try and figure out what the Greys had done to them. Along this whole process from 1954 onward, the MAJIC-12 military-government was trying to act like Meiji-Restoration Japan, **[32C]** that is, trying to copy and re-create all of the most advanced Alien Foreign-Power military technology as fast as possible so that one day we might have a real fighting chance against these foreign space-invaders. In this way the MAJIC-12 group may be viewed as 'Grey-Hats'. It's easy to Monday-morning quarterback here, and there was probably a more RIGHTEOUS AEON path forward, but they did what they thought was necessary. In this case it resulted in the medical-mutilation of at least thousands of American civilians, giving the Aliens a toe-hold on the planet in joint Alien-human Deep Underground Bases, and a slow-walk cooption of the entire United States Government **[37H]** through the use of Clones and brain-chip-implantation by off-world Foreign Powers. [Return-of-the-Body-Snatcher's type takeover]

It may be useful and clarifying to view the situation from the perspective of The Orion Empire. Each one of these agreements reached with a particular group of humans represents a leverage-point in the politics of earth that may be exploited in an attempt to mold the Terran Civilization to Orion-Alien Imperial goals. Certain agreements were probably reached with the League of Nations and French Secretary-General Joseph Avenol 1928-1933; certain agreements reached with the Germans 1925-1945; certain agreements reached with the US military-government MAJIC-12 1947-1954; additional agreements have probably been reached with certain corporations or other powerful individuals. In every case these are secret Faustian contracts which serve to coopt a portion of the power-structure of Terran Civilization to Alien ends. **[37H]** To the average civilian on earth the sum of these coopted power-structures feels like a Secret-Government, a Shadow-Government, a Deep-State, or a Cabal. If you ask too many questions about it their representatives, the Men-In-Black show up at your door and tell you to shut up. If you see too much they wipe your brains with Will Smith's little flashy-thing from MIB-1. Secrecy has been used by the Orion Aliens to try to prevent the General Population of earth from perceiving the origin of the threat; **[37H]** and compartmentalization has been used to limit the sight-picture of each coopted military, government, or corporate group.

MAJIC-12 and these other coopted departments can still come to Jesus. The council made the agreements with the Greys in 1954 **[A31]** **[12L]** so the council can renounce the agreements now. Who knows, maybe this kind of stalling-tactic, 70 years in the making now, really has produced sufficient Space-Age military-defense advancement that we may now thumb our nose at the Orion Aliens, burn the Faustian contracts and come clean about what mistakes were made in a previous generation under duress. US Army Military-Intelligence Colonel Phillip Corso **[9I]** said that his higher-ranking friends in the military (MAJIC-12) had been forced into a kind of negotiated-surrender to the Aliens. Most of the original council-members that made those agreements in a state a fear and in a time of uncertainty are now dead. Their modern replacements can simply say,

"Our predecessors were wrong. We renounce the agreements they made. When we were read-in to these seats behind a veil of secrecy we had no idea what had been going on. It is clear now that our predecessors were

deceived by the Orion Greys and the contracts they entered into were inherently immoral; we renounce those contracts categorically, even at the risk of our own lives, on behalf of all American citizens and the peoples of earth. We stand in solidarity with all mankind in this matter and wholeheartedly believe that now, more than ever, we are able to stand up to the Alien threat. Mankind as a whole is strong and innovative, and it is in fact the Aliens that are afraid of us and not the other way round."

I'm sure that the General Public and outer-court of Military Intelligence officers will understand if the current MAJIC-12 Council comes clean in this manner. We can simply blame any previous mis-steps on a previous generation of Boomers who seemingly got everything else wrong as well. At any rate our future leadership needs to come clean and publicly renounce these secret Faustian contracts, burning their effigy in public in order to welcome in a new RIGHTEOUS AEON.

The Orion Group

"Canst thou bind the sweet influences of Pleiades, or loose the bands of Orion?"

— Book of Job 38:31 KJV

Often termed "negative-ETs" because of their constant complaining The Orion Group is composed of several separate species working together in an interconnected Galactic Empire, with generally the Reptoids being the bosses. The species which compose The Orion Group include, but are not limited to: The Reptilians, The Zeta-Reticuli Greys, The Insectalids, and The Nacht Waffen Space-NAZIs as described below:

The Reptoids "Space-Dragons"

The first and foremost of the sentient species of The Orion Group worth mentioning are the Reptoids. Blame God for creating a reptile Alien, but they are much as their name would imply: Predatory. Carnivorous. Lacking in empathy. Somewhat in personality akin to Arnold Schwarzenegger's Alien in *"The Predator"* movie from 1987. In the past the Reptilians actually did and have used Earth as a kind of 'happy hunting-grounds' giving rise to many of our most ancient legends regarding certain types of monsters. The Reptilians are aggressive, expansionist, bent on conquest and enslavement of as many foreign planets, species, and peoples as possible. [A31] They are prideful, preferring to be called what translates into English something like, 'the Royal Draconians'. They hail generally from planets orbiting the star systems we would classify as the Orion Constellation. Their societies are based primarily on power, domination, and the use of force or threat of force. Naked force and coercion is hard-baked into their chains of command, maybe somewhat like a Fascist NAZI-type situation. That being said they do respect Force, and the use of Force. In their view species that will not stick up for themselves are prey-animals that deserve to be enslaved. Terrans have some of the strongest Life-Force in the known universe, which to Reptoid taste makes them the most tasty of all delicacies. Kind of like how we might view a 3,000-lb long-horn bull. We envision the hundreds of tasty steaks he will make. That's more-or-less the Reptoid view of the Terrans. [3C]

The Zeta-Reticuli "Greys"

The second sentient species of The Orion Group worth mentioning, due to their now extensive interactions with mankind, are the Zeta-Reticuli, the little Grey Aliens. So named by us in English "Zeta-Reticuli" due to their star-system of origin, Zeta-Reticuli. The Zeta-Reticuli are a conquered species. Conquered by the Reptilians. As such they can be expected to more-or-less carry out the will of their Reptilian overlords at a strategic level. Their original home-world was destroyed by the Reptilians and they were forced to relocate to Planet Serpo **[18R]**. Culturally the Zeta Reticuli living on Planet Serpo have a society comparable to North Korea. Government and Military technology is at a (comparatively to us) high level of advancement. Yet the vast majority of Greys live in the most basic of austere of conditions, often lacking even centralized heating and cooling for their personal domiciles, lacking all but the most basic forms of entertainment and culture. The 12 Astronauts sent to Planet Serpo in the 1960s observed the Greys arraigning themselves standing in groups in the public square during non-work hours in creative shapes as a form of entertainment, kind of like a live-action Tetris-game, for example. This was pretty much the high-watermark of Zeta-Reticuli 'arts and culture'. Their day was governed by a strict work-schedule based off of a type of centralized town sun-dial, central to each village or town. No TV, no video games, no plays, no art, no cards, no gambling, no drugs, no alcohol, no guns, no clubs, no bars, no strippers, no restaurants, no churches, no hookers, no computers dedicated to entertainment or cultural purposes. No elaborate forms of cooking. No X-box. Their society is essentially a military dictatorship similar to a North-Korea type situation with ultimately the Reptilians telling them what to do at the top. **[3C] [18R]**

The genetic devolution of the Zeta Reticuli has to do with their spiritual, moral, and ethical degradation over many hundreds or thousands of years. You see, the Zeta Reticuli are culturally obsessed with cloning and gene-splicing of all sentient races, animals, plants, and themselves with all of the above. **[18R]** This has created a cosmic freak-show of every conceivable combination of being, like Groot from the Avengers, and more on the way. But that is the least of their problems. Because for the most part they have abandoned natural sexual-reproduction and natural birth in favor of artificial cloning chambers over many generations, this has caused some problems for them. For starters it eliminates most or all of the spiritual creation process that is actually a contributing part of natural reproduction. We probably don't appreciate the positive benefits of this spiritual life-force role in natural reproduction very much because we've always had it and have never been without it until very recently. But the Zeta Reticuli have gone without it for many generations in some or all of their lines, and it causes a kind of devolution of the genetics over time. It is an artificial process and may perhaps be likened unto a legacy document at the office where you lost the original a long time ago, and so you just keep copying the last copy whenever you get low on that form to the bottom of the stack, and this has been going on for years now. Eventually the originally straight-lincs of your original form start to droop and warp hideously. Legacy spots start to appear and then grow bigger and weirder with each successive generation of copies. You've all done this around the office and know exactly what I'm talking about. Well, that's what the Zeta Reticuli are suffering from. But they are so culturally obsessed with the cloning process itself, it is like their crown-jewel of technology, like how Americans think about Nukes, -that now they can't stop, because it is cultural now for them and totally endemic to their societies, like a kind of obsession. So they go around the universe slurping up other races of animals, plants, and sentient life, like humans, to gene-splice and recombine. **[18R]**

The Zeta Reticuli, when they think about 'warfare' think about 3 critical components: Cloning, Infiltration, and Mind Control. This is perhaps not the way we would conceptualize warfare as Americans or as Earthlings, but it has led the Zeta Reticuli species to success in the past over other planets, and therefor they are capitalizing on their past successes.

The Zeta Reticuli possess powerful latent Mind-abilities that are not scientific, but are rather species-specific brain-characteristics of this particular ET. **[20T] [27Z]** It is not all-powerful, but as with any manipulation it is even more effective if the victim is not aware of its influence. The Zeta Reticuli have the ability to plant thoughts and ideas, speaking directly into the mind of the victim. This can range from complex political concepts like population-control, to individual direct-action promptings like jumping off of a bridge. Do you see why the Zeta Reticuli don't really need Nukes? Instead, they focus on Mind-War as the primary means of manipulation and control. **[20T]** **[27Z]** By contrast, they are culturally averse to guns and bombs as tools of war, **[18R]** viewing them as barbaric, probably instilled into them by their Reptilian overlords as a mechanism of control, as they are now a slave-class of the Draco-Reptilian Empire, The Orion Group. For this same reason the Greys almost certainly do not possess nuclear weapons, or similar bombs of mass-destruction, as that would remain a latent threat to their Draco-Reptilian Overlords.

During our Astronaut-Exchange program of 1962 to Planet Serpo the Zeta-Reticuli killed our Chief Security Officer, one of 12 men, by prompting him to jump off of a bridge through Mind-War. **[18R]** The Airforce Security Officer had previously threatened his Zeta-Reticuli Hosts with retaliation with guns and bombs in connection with the death or killing of one of the other Astronauts during spaceflight to Planet Serpo. **[18R]** The Zeta-Reticuli Mind Powers were not well understood at the time, and both deaths were essentially ruled as accidental by the Airforce, but in reviewing the documents currently available more than a half-century later, the Zeta Reticuli probably killed at least 2, or as many as 4 of the exchange-Astronauts intentionally. The first Astronaut was killed during interstellar spaceflight to Planet Serpo. He was probably intentionally killed by the Zeta-Reticuli for scientific research purposes, as his remains and DNA were meticulously dissected by them, and then re-purposed in order to create a series of Grey/Human hybrid clones. The mission's Security-Officer was probably carefully killed during a period of isolation from the rest of the Team by Mind-War. We now know that the Zeta-Reticuli meticulously, rigorously, and repetitively train for Mind-War, specifically with the tactic of inducing a human victim to hurl themselves off of a high precipice or bridge. **[20T]** **[27Z]** The power of this type of deadly Mind-War is not absolute, but it is certainly more effective if the victim is not aware of its influence. As only 8 of 12 Astronauts returned from the exchange program back to Earth from Planet Serpo, the deaths of 2 and the non-return of 2 more for a total of 4 are highly suspect. Inhuman treatment of humans by the Zeta-Reticuli is a reoccurring political reality thoroughly documented many times over the last century that should not be forgotten moving forward in our negotiations with them and their masters, The Orion Group. [18R] [20T] [27Z]

The Insectalids "Talking Preying-Mantis"

Insect-like hominid race focused on the wonders of Science. They have a focus on consciousness-transfer technology, especially for humans. Generally the Zeta-Reticuli Grey Aliens will take care of the physical cloning-process of a human, whilst the Insectalids will complete the process with a soul-split to place a soul-fragment of the original in the new clone. The clone was grown from its inception with a computer chip in its head for total tracking and control. The new clone may then be used as a Super-Soldier, Slave, or Puppet of The Orion Group. They tend to be sort of intellectual-mercenaries, scientifically-oriented, and morally neutral. Other than that they have a pretty good sense of humor.

The Nacht Waffen "Space NAZIs"

Last but not least, and sadly lacking a sense of humor, we also have the Nacht Waffen "Dark Fleet" as part of The Orion Group. "Space-NAZIs". [4D] [8H] [30Z] [A31] The good news is that mankind has already reached many a distant star-system and habitable M-class planet, by the use of advanced technologies given by Aliens, for which I suppose we might feel quite proud. The bad news is that most of them are direct bloodline and ideological descendants of the Waffen-SS, [8H] [4D] [30Z] and they Nuked a lot of the other planets they visited. Thus, patching things up with some of the other planets and civilizations in the future might be a challenge.

You see, the Reptilians prefer to rule by proxy. [3C] They were once upon a time certainly great warriors, but somewhat like the Roman Empire in its waning years, they have tended to rely more and more heavily upon Mercenaries. This is a kind of natural devolution of Empires in general. After a certain period of Imperial greatness, hard-won by the soldiers thereof, the peoples of the expanding Empire often decide they don't want to be front-line shock-troops anymore, like the Romans, like the British. And in this state-of-mind will tend to hire more and more German Mercenaries to play the role of front-line shock-troops to be killed in the front lines of battle. Several of our Earth-Empires made this same decision with regards specifically to the German people. First, the Roman Empire recruited and used a lot of German Mercenaries in its war-machine, especially in the later-half of the Empire. The British Empire did it again in the mid to late 1700s, which is why we here in America still remember fighting German 'Hessians', -mercenaries of the British Empire during the American Revolutionary War. Apparently the German people make good mercenaries for whatever reason. Well, the Reptoids did it again over the last 100 years for their intergalactic Empire too. As they performed their planetary assessment of Earth, its peoples, and resources, the Reptoids incorrectly assessed the Germans to be the apex 'master race' of the humans. They were incorrect about this, however, as it is actually the *Italians.* -who invented Pizza? *Italians.* Who invented Lasagna? *Italians.* Who took over the city of New York with gangsters? *Italians.* Who founded Las Vegas? *Italians.* Who painted the Sistine-Chapel? *Italians.* Who chiseled Michelangelo's David? *Italians.* Who invented the first helicopter? *Italians.* Who forged the Roman Empire? *Italians.* Who built the Vatican? *Italians.* Who had the first secret-space program? *Italians.* I rest my case. Italians are the true master-race, the Reptilians got it all wrong.

The Reptilians think in terms of a pecking-order, after all, with themselves at the top of the peck. [3C] In this strategic-plan for planet earth the Reptoids would back the 'German-master-race' with advanced technology, weapons, and intelligence. The Germans were supposed to take over all of the European continent to form a super-state, and dominate the other Europeans. The European super-state would then rule-over and dominate the rest of Planet Earth going forward. The Reptoids would dominate the Germans in a pyramidal command-and-control structure, and the planet would be conquered. They had used this basic pyramidal command-and-control structure on other conquered planets in the past. We remember this in history as the World War-2 period. All did not go according to plan here on earth, however, and the combined activities of the British, American, and Russian tribes defeated the Reptoid-backed German faction in what we now remember as World War 2. But the Reptoid planners did not completely abandon this line-of-effort even though it failed. If you've ever been on a military staff or a corporate board-room planning team you'll know exactly what I'm talking about: some people just refuse to admit the failure of their bad ideas. They just keep on harping on their same old failed policies and lines of effort over and over again and throwing more money at it. No matter how spectacular the failure they just keep chewing on the ends of their old plots, as if to say: 'I'm really not an idiot! you'll see! it'll work out in the end if we just keep at it!' And so you pour even more time, focus, energy, and money into the same old product lines that failed before. Same thing here. Even though Reptilian-backed Germany lost the war, some of the Reptoid officers just couldn't admit defeat. They tried to salvage the remains of their failed project by transporting several-thousand pure-blood-pedigree wounded-Waffen-SS soldiers to secret bases in Antarctica (and elsewhere in the cosmos) along with about X3 'racially-pure' Ukraine slave-girls as long-term breeding-stock for them. Some of this dark comedy made its way into films like *'Dr. Strangelove' - 1964*. But ultimately this was a Reptilian plan, enabled by Reptilian ideas, intelligence, technology, and resources. Thus a section of German descendants became a kind of high-tech mercenary-force of the Draco-Reptilian Empire, today known as the 'Nacht Waffen' in German, or 'the Dark Fleet' in English. **[8H] [4D] [30Z] [3C]**

Coop-some, kill the rest. Just like General Patton, in one man's view the Nacht Waffen should probably be wooed back into the Earthling fold as a long-term strategy. They should be reminded that their racial and ancestral kinship is a thousand-times more closely aligned to the rest of the Terrans of planet earth than Reptiles from Alpha-Draconis. This type of negotiation-strategy will become more and more a possibility as the strength of US Space Force, US Navy-Space, and Space-X increases. We have to present the generational exiles of the Nacht-Waffen with a strong space-force, worthy of coming home to as a long-term strategic goal. The alternative is that the Reptilian Empire will use the Nacht-Waffen fleet against us and the other emerging space-forces of Earth and we'll be fighting Space-NAZIs again.

The Pyramid & the Eye

"You're One Ugly Motherfucker!"
– Dutch (Arnold Schwarzenegger) to the Predator,
The Predator 1987

Unfortunately, there have been a number of attempts by The Orion Group to try and take over the world. Earth the planet has been a jewel in the crown of The Orion Empire for quite some time, at least from their point of view. [3C] Maybe somewhat like Russia thinks about Ukraine, or the Dutch used to think about South Africa. Even if the Orions had not been ruling earth overtly in broad-daylight since Reptilian Lord Quetzalcoatl, they still considered it to be rightfully theirs both as a big-game happy hunting grounds (of humans) and for its mineral and biological resources (of humans). These aims had been somewhat thwarted by the Galactic Federation of Worlds and the Pleiadeans over thousands of years that thought the peoples of earth needed to develop independently without being molested by other Outer-Space-Civilizations. Nevertheless, the Orion-Group and Reptoids persisted with a certain amount of infiltration [27Z] [3C] of earth-societies over the centuries despite Federation and Pleiadean cock-blocking. The Reptoids cultivated their power-nucleuses especially within the Satanic-Secret-Societies with whom they had always been in-contact for thousands of years, [3C] the Christian and Muslim perception of the situation being not too far off the mark. [For Westerners: a significant portion of Muslim scholars believe that many governments

74

are being controlled by Satan through illuminati secret societies, with ideas similar to Christian Conspiracy-Theorists]

With the advent of the Nuclear-Age in 1945 the Orion-Group and Reptoid Aliens stepped up their earth-infiltration-operations a thousand-fold, which is their primary modus-operandi for taking down rival civilizations. [A31] They could see that the civilizations of earth would soon become both spacefaring and nuclear-powers to be reckoned with in the near-future if allowed to continue on un-checked and un-controlled. The Orions & Reptoids performed detailed and comprehensive surveys of Earth political-systems to see how they might be exploited to their aims. Continuing with the infiltration-ethic they decided they would use a combination of Strategies that had worked on many other developing planetary civilizations before. Starting in the 1920s they would use a combination of Faustian-contracts with key-human-leader-groups, like the German Thule Society, [30Z] The League of Nations under French Secretary-General Joseph Avenol, and in America with the MAJIC-12 military-government. [A31] These Faustian-contracts were predicated upon bribery with advanced technologies along with an implicit threat of force. Something similar to the Faustian-contracts that the Europeans had made with the Kings of the Ivory Coast with "guns for souls". Yet to this the Orions and Reptoids would add Cloning of key human leaders in deep underground bases [11K] [25Y] in some tens-of-thousands as large-scale operations to replace any key-leaders that might need to be replaced, something like an advanced version of the CIA/KGB infiltration and political-takeover model. [33D] And to that they would add mind-control and brain-chip-implantation for total tracking and control of their human mind-thralls, similar to the Nura-Link Elon Musk likes to brag about. As an additional strategy of cooption and control they would add a "When in Rome" corruption strategy to key human-leaders with Adrenochrome-addiction. Most of the Reptoids are Adrenochrome-addicts themselves so this would have the added benefit of binding the human Adrenochrome-addicts to the off-world Reptoid Adrenochrome-addicts in common-cause. A certain amount of human child-abduction & harvesting is necessary to support this industry as the drug uses human blood (with lifeforce within) as a base-element, to which they add synthetic opiates. That would be carried out by the Deep-State managerial-class in a similar manner to the way the Kings of the Ivory coast used advanced European-Alien weapons to capture more and more slaves from the interior of Africa and sell them back to the European-Aliens as an analogy. The managerial-class junkies and institutions of human key-leaders that became corrupted and controlled by these processes over the last 100 years time we would probably call "The Deep State" or "The Cabal". In reality it is Orion-Group and Reptoid intervention and management at the very top of the pyramid of control. To these several strategies of global-domination would be added the manufacture & release of super-viruses like COVID-19 in order to reduce Earth's population down to a manageable number. The vaccines manufactured by the Deep-State & Cabal to supposedly inoculate the General Public from the Super-Virus releases would themselves have additional trojan-horses of self-assembling nanites, sterilization-poisons, mutagens, mind-altering properties, and tracking devices, just like the ones you all just took. Although the reduction of the non-cynical human population may itself have unintended consequences as they have created a natural-selection scenario in which only the most Conspiratorial and Paranoid of the humans remain standing.

As of 2024 we are now in a process of sort of hacking our way up the Alien-Reptoid-Orion-Monster from the toes up. Confronting the Clones, chip-implanted, mind-thralls, and Adrenochrome-addicts, harvesters, peddlers, manufacturers, and distributors at the very bottom of the pyramid-of-control first. But we have to also understand this is the very beginning of the process. There is a lot of corrupted Adrenochrome-addicted human-Cabal and brain-chip-implanted Deep-State-Clone managerial class in the middle before actually getting all the way up to Reptoid shapeshifters and Nebu-Greys who manage the whole thing at the top on a global-scale. This is sort of the apex of what Alex-Jones used to perceive as "Globalists" from underneath the pyramid-of-control groping his way up.

It is actually an Outer-Space-Alien invasion. **[3C] [11K] [13M] [20T] [27Z] [27W] [28X] [A31] [37H]** But rather than an "Independence-Day" style invasion with Death-Ray vaporization of the White-House, it is more of a "Return-of-the-Body-Snatchers" type invasion, slow, stealthy, creeping-death of the human population over time; at least that's what the Orions are trying to do. The end-result is kind of up to you I guess. If like an Ostrich you stick your head back in the sand because it's scary and decide there's no such thing as Aliens, no such thing as clones, no such thing as brain-chips, no such thing as the Deep-State, no such thing as the Cabal, no such thing as mind-control, no such thing as Adrenochrome, no such thing as Superviruses; you're going to get bum-rushed by the Reptoid-Komoto-dragon metaphorically-speaking, and you will only have yourself to blame. If on the other hand you get active, spreading knowledge and awareness of the true Cosmic situation to your fellow-Terrans as we all learn together, we stand a pretty good chance of beating this outer-space invasion and coming out victorious.

The Killer Rabbit of Caerbannog

"look at its fangs!"
– Monty Python and the Holy Grail, 1975

The Aliens are now in a state of panic. The looming lift-off of mankind to the stars weighs heavy upon their minds, even in a weightless environment. The terrible Ontological-shock to them regarding what Tesla and Oppenheimer and Jesus Christ have already done is only just now fully setting in. Like when Dr. Frankenstein realized that his monster had gotten out of control. Like when you finally realize a gofer infestation has taken over your front-lawn. Like when you realize your wife invited over the entire 6th grade class for your son's birthday party. Processes have been set in motion that cannot now be reversed. The Gorilla's got the key to the zoo, the key is Nuclear Science, and now the Gorillas are tossing the key back-and-forth from one Gorilla to the other Gorilla, with the Alien zoo-keepers playing Monkey-in-the-Middle.

As mankind we hold a number of unique characteristics that actually make us quite dangerous to the Aliens. It's hard for us to be objective here. I mean, we're us, and we've never not been us, so to be like us and behave as we do seems natural because it's all we've ever known. But to the Aliens we're really weird.

In comparison to the Pleiadeans, Reptoids, and Anunnaki we have a really high birth-rate. Our generations turn over every 15-20 years or so. I don't know what High School you went to. In just 15-20 years you can have a whole new generation of fast-learning violent humans on your hands, just like that, like rows of shark's-teethe replacing one another. That's how the Pleiadeans, Reptoids, and Anunnaki view us, like rows of baby-shark teethe constantly being re-formed and growing up fast to maturity. Even if theoretically you were to vaporize the whole current generation of adult Terrans in a Thanos-Snap, our kids would grow up to maturity in just a decade or so, like Inigo Montoya from the Princess-Bride and seek revenge. From the Pleiadean, Reptoid, and Anunnaki perspective we breed like rabbits, but we are not just a passive herb-eating prey-animal rabbit. Quite the opposite, we are like an exponentially multiplying infestation of militant, carnivorous, dissatisfied, angry rabbits with fangs like the Killer Rabbit of Caerbannog from Monty-Python. Innocent looking enough, perhaps, but concealing a voracious bite.

Do you remember that one Star-Trek-Next-Generation episode where they encounter this genetically-enhanced super-soldier that's all badass and creative and uses his shuttle to bounce off the shields of the Enterprise and escape and he's like a space-MacGyver on steroids in terms of his tactics to the point where the Enterprise crew have a hard time catching up with him? (*Star Trek: The Next Generation, Episode 59 "The Hunted"*) That's basically how the real Galactic Federation views American military personnel. Psychologically programmed in Boot Camp to follow orders and kill on command, tactically creative, resilient. In the Star Trek episode after fighting wars on behalf of his people and government, he then ends up with PTSD and is not fit to integrate back into civilian society. But just as is illustrated in the Star Trek episode, despite our inferior technology, the Federation Aliens are often surprised by our martial prowess. They are intimidated by our superior Stoiyl. In this allegory the "Angosians" and their planet actually represent the Terrans and planet Earth, more specifically the Americans, more specifically American Soldiers, and the Enterprise crew actually represents the Galactic Federation of Worlds. That is basically how the Federation Aliens view Terran Soldiers and military personnel, especially Americans even in their regular stock-models in terms of being super-soldiers, even with no genetic engineering, but then you can upgrade them with cybernetic implants and certain genetic modifications if you want. The Aliens view us kind of like the stock-model of an American Corvette. It's already pretty badass just the way it is, but you can also add fancy rims, a custom paint-job, and a flow-master plus or NOS if you want.

The 'genetic enhancements' and the bad-treatment of the super-soldier by his government in Star-Trek TNG episode 59 represents modifications that are sometimes performed in Terran black-ops groups, also by Reptilians and by Greys. However, it also more generally refers to the brutality (from the Federation point of view) of our military-training processes, i. e. Bootcamps, that we Terrans embrace as a normal and beneficial aspect of our martial-culture. I've been on both sides of the fence here, both as a trainee and a trainer several times. I believe our Boot Camps are a unique integral and powerful aspect of our Martial Culture here on Holy Terra that should be upheld. Just like in Star Trek TNG episode 59, the real Galactic Federation of Worlds views our military Boot-Camps as regressive psychological conditioning programs that program into our troops the ability to kill on command, which of course they are. This also means that we can escape becoming absorbed by the Galactic Federation of Worlds by maintaining or increasing the brutality of our military boot-camps which would be unacceptable to their delicate Space-Elf sensibilities. I'm counting on the Drill Sergeant Corps of all Terran nations to maintain standards in this regard.

Also of note in the same TNG Star-Trek episode is that empathic counselor Troy (who represents Pleiadean Empaths) does not detect negative or 'bad vibes' from the captured super-soldier despite the fact that he injured the security team during his attempted escape. This mirrors the empathic Pleiadean and Federation sentiment that they generally get from Terrans 'positive' or 'good-vibes' in the context of their own spirituality despite the fact that we are from their perspective observably hyper-violent. These sentiments feed into the Federation idea that Terrans will make good front-line shock-troops for them to prosecute their wars against the Orion Empire in the future, and then return home to make sweet love to them afterward, even though our overweening observed militancy gives them pause. [A31]

When we find out that the Pleiadeans live about 700 years, and Reptoids about 600 years, and Anunnaki for thousands of years, and we only live about 70 years we might feel diminished, inferior even, especially when we learn that Social Security just ran out. But that's not the way the Pleiadeans and Reptoids and Anunnaki look at it. We have short lives, yes, but we also learn really fast. It's kind of like the difference between how fast a teenager learns verses how fast your 87-year-old great-uncle learns. Now just expand that out to a 500-year-old, 600-year-old, or 700-year-old Pleiadean, Reptoid, or Anunnaki. As Professor Tolkien said prophetically: *they attempted nothing new*. Yet humans are attempting new things in every generation all the time. We like to think big. As a matter-of-fact each of our generations tend to have different proclivities. So even if the Pleiadeans or Reptoids or Anunnaki have a short-term success in indoctrinating one of our generations with crunchie-granola-hippie-peace-light-and-love like the dope-smoking Boomer Generation, it almost doesn't even matter because you can just as easily have a militant Christian-or-Muslim-Imperial generation like the Zoomers or Alphas coming up just 20-40 years right after it. From the Pleiadean or Reptoid or Anunnaki perspective that's like the blink of an eye.

Also, as Terrans we like to fight and Nuke each other. **[A31]** I know this may not seem odd to you because chances are if you're reading this book you are another Terran like me and we are just conditioned to having a history and present-day chalk-full of inter-tribal warfare: war-books, weapons of war, Maori Warriors on Surfboards etc . . If we're not currently involved with some type of military conflict we feel uneasy and bored. Well, all of the other Alien races aren't like that. They don't all like war as much as we do. The Zeta-Reticuli for example, the little Grey Aliens, are just chicken-necked nerds by comparison that don't like guns just like your 2nd grade elementary-school teacher. A lot of the different Alien races we would consider to be Pacifists, especially on the Galactic Federation of World's side. **[12L]** In this respect we Terrans are more akin to the *Star-Trek Mirror-Verse Federation*, or *Starship Troopers*. Even the Reptoids who are quite cunning and mean-spirited most of the time are still not prepared to fight and die in front-line combat as Shock-Troops, while conversely a lot of our Terran young men are. A lot of us can't wait to fight and die in front-line-combat on a distant world, in fact we love it. Like Colonel Kurts in *Apocalypse Now* a lot of us love the smell of Napalm in the morning and view all this talk about peace and happiness as a lot of dope-smoking nonsense. Do you see the problem? Because the Aliens sure do. From the Alien perspective we are hyper-violent, hyper-militant, and yet still smart enough to pilot space-ships, shoot laser-beams, and lob Nukes at anyone we don't like. Plus violent militant warlords like yours truly and prophet Joshua are influencing you and they can't figure out how to make it stop.

The Reptoids seem to be the first Extraterrestrial race to intuit the ramifications of this woeful state of affairs. The first ones to realize our 'Rabbit of Caerbannog' potential. Probably because they had been big-game hunting us for millennia. Much like a Britisher or American will go on an African Safari to Zimbabwe to hunt Cecil the Black-Maned Lion. And why would we hunt Cecil the Black-Maned Lion? Why would we hunt another carnivorous animal? We don't even usually eat lion's meat. So what really is the point of hunting Cecil the Black-Maned Lion like we do? The whole point is to prove man's dominance over nature, to prove our dominance over the wild beast, to prove our dominance over another super-predator. For the same reason that some of our American and Mexican men see how long they can ride Bulls that don't want to be ridden. For the same reason that the Spanish Matador skewers Ferdinand the Friendly Bull. The whole point is as if to say, *'see! WE the humans are really the apex predator, WE are the real kings of the jungle because we killed the greatest other king of the jungle, Cecil the Black-Maned Lion, and made him into a coat for my girlfriend! So there! We rode Ferdinand the Friendly Bull even though he didn't want to be ridden! Take that!'* The whole point is to prove the superiority of man. In like manner, and for the same reason, the Reptoid big-game hunters have gone on Safari to Earth the jungle-world and hunted man on Earth for thousands of years. Kind of like the Hunger Games, or Arnold Schwarzenegger's Predator, to prove to themselves and to one-another that they really are the greatest of the apex predators of the universe. To turn us into coats for their girlfriends. To collect our bronze-age artifacts in private collections and Reptoid museums just like the British used to do. Much as is depicted in Arnold Schwarzenegger's "Predator" film 1987, the Reptoids have been hunting man for a long time, many thousands of years. So long in fact that it has become the subject of many of our most terrifying monster-legends regarding the legend of the dragon, and some of our most cherished heroic epics, like the Legend of Beowulf.

Because the Reptoids are predators themselves and have hunted man, they recognized and in a way respected the predatory nature of man, as king of our own jungle, in the same way the African Safari Big-Game Hunters recognize the predatory nature of Cecil the Black-Maned Lion. As a kind of compliment almost. Much more so than say the Pleiadeans who are by nature Pacifist. This is a case of 'it-takes-one-to-know-one'. We're not prey-animals like deer or Elk or Pleiadeans that run away from a fight as a first line of defense, but rather we often stand and fight, or perhaps even initiate the fight ourselves as a first resort. Sometimes we call this a 'preemptive-first-strike' doctrine. Thus, the Reptoid response to man's technological development was and has been to give us even more weapons, to coopt our latent warrior energies rolled into and under the command-and-control of their own Empire, The Orion Group. Rather than attempting to eradicate Terrans as we might suspect or fear, the Reptilian response has always been to attempt to coopt our destiny and latent powers to their own designs, in an Imperial fashion, sort of like the Roman Empire. Therefor the Reptoids were also the first to develop humans as Super-Soldiers for service in their own intergalactic armies. **[A31] [37H] [8H] [4D] [30Z]**

The next big intervention by the Reptoids on Earth began in the 1920s, with several German mentalists of the Thule society making first psychic-contact, and then later physical-contact with the Reptoids of The Orion Empire. **[30Z]** Much of German Eugenics ideology from that period was probably an externalization of the method of Reptoid *survival* *of the fittest'* ideology. Through this mechanism the Reptoids were able to feed the Germans technology and over-the-horizon intelligence information to aid them in their wars against the rest of the world. We remember this in history as the World-War-2 period where Germany tried to take over the world. **[4D] [8H] [30Z] [3C]**

The Reptoids would keep their presence on Earth a secret for the same reason a crocodile lurks just below the surface of the water at the edge of the watering-hole on an African Savannah: He's waiting to pop out and devour the first unsuspecting Wildabeast that wanders by. So no one could ever expect Disclosure from the Reptoids. However, the reasoning going on in the brains of the Pleiadeans and Galactic Federation of Worlds people is a little bit more complex. They are supposed to be the 'good' Aliens, right? So why don't they reveal themselves so mankind can have a clue about what is really going on? I will explain:

Because of these powerful latent energies contained within the Terran race, the Aliens are using a lot of delaying tactics to try and slow us down. Both the Reptoids *and* the Pleiadeans. For their part the Pleiadeans and the Galactic Federation of Worlds would have wanted a lot more time (many more centuries) before we get loose in the cosmos to Disarm, Pacify, Ingratiate, Litigate, Ally-with, and Intermarry with us than they actually have. That's why they haven't landed on the 50 yard line during the Superbowl. They don't really want a mass-awakening of the General Terran population any faster than it already is. If we all freak out when confronted by the true cosmic situation in our current psychological and spiritual state, they know we will claw our way up the tech-tree with a quickness giving rise to something like a spacefaring and nuclear-armed Taliban (in their view). The situation may be likened unto the way Feudal Japan quickly adopted Western Technology from 1870-1900 without any accompanying societal transformation, and then started beating European Westerners at their own game with the spirit of the Samurai in full-force and then forged a diesel-punk Empire in their own right up until the present-day. **[32C]** In history we call this the Meiji Restoration. **[32C]** That is the type of situation the Galactic Federation of Worlds foresees and fears in all their over-the-horizon computer simulation models, and are desperately trying to avoid. Thus, they really don't want the rest of planet earth developing any faster than it is already because we automatically turn any and all new technological developments into weapons. [A31] Which is exactly why we pushed up the Disclosure Timeline and forced the issue way faster than any of the Alien groups wanted. The battle for the Disclosure Timeline isn't between Congress and the Pentagon, it's between the People of Earth and the Aliens themselves. They are desperately (and now unsuccessfully) trying to control our psychological paradigm of what is and isn't real, and the amount of knowledge and technology we are exposed to, precisely because our rate of learning, copying, and inventing is so fast from their point of view, like Japanese people. [32C] For Mankind, and especially Germans, Britishers, Japanese, [32C] Russians, and Americans, possesses a type of 'Mental Adrenaline' that causes us to invent new types of weapons when threatened. -Just like we all did during the World War 2 conflict when fighting each other. [32C]

To more fully understand the situation you have to look at it from the Alien point of view. It behooves them to keep the largest portion of Earth's population ignorant of their presence for as long as possible. [3C] [8H] [20T] [27Z] The moment a majority of the Earth's population realizes there's a whole Galaxy out there to conquer — it puts Alien lives in jeopardy. This is why the Pleiadeans talk about Earthlings not being ready for the Space-Age with the spirit of conquest and the Nukes we have now. The Nukes are actually a Space-Age weapon a thousand years ahead of their time we invented due to our latent 'mental-adrenaline' capacity during World War 2 under threat of the Alien technology that had already been given to the Germans. Instead, The idea here is to keep the majority of the Earth's population ignorant of the Alien Intervention, even as it is ongoing, for as long as possible while they puppet-master and try to play one earth-tribe off against the other. The Pleiadeans have to walk a fine-line here because they are trying to play the 'good-cop' / 'big-sister' role -they have to make it look like they are trying to come clean and disclose themselves to the General Public of Earth at the earliest possible moment, even as they slow-walk it for as long as possible. They don't want anyone to ask later, (effect country-Western accent here) "why didn't ya'll just land a spaceship on the 50-yard line of the Superbowl at halftime? And walk down the gang-plank like Mr. Spock?" < it will be interesting to see their response. But we already know the reason. The Pleiadeans and the Galactic Federation of Worlds Aliens actually don't want Disclosure or man's awareness of an Alien presence on Earth to progress any faster than it already is or they would have done that a hundred years ago when football was still called Rugby. Such a shock to the human psyche would probably allow violent war-lords such as myself to take over the narrative and harness mankind's latent energies to destructive ends, -a grave risk to just about everyone in the universe. On the other hand, the Pleiadeans and Galactic Federation of Worlds Aliens have been engaged in limited Contact with select individuals for the purpose of trying to disarm all our Nukes and so that they can falsely claim later that they made every effort to effect Disclosure to the General Population at the earliest possible moment even as in reality they slow-walk it for as long as possible.

You see, this whole thing is just a test of our resolve. As President Franklin D. Roosevelt said who won World War 2 for the American-Terrans: *We have nothing to fear, but fear itself*". Why do you think all these Reptoids and Greys and Pleiadeans and Anunnaki have been pussie-footing around for the last 100 years, slithering in and out of the shadows, . . . it's because they know that when the Honey-Badger gets angry its hell to pay. Now's not the time to snivel into your corn flakes. It's time to get the spirit of the Templar, Samurai, and Mujahadeen in Nuclear-Armed Warp-Fighters with the Tanakh, Koran, Book-of-Five-Rings and the Apocalypse of John tattooed on their foreheads and just let 'em have it. It's precisely this prospect that makes the Aliens fear for their lives, -quake in their magnetic boots, and foresee a mighty Cataclysm for themselves of Galactic proportions. **[12L]**

~~Don't~~ Panic! The Fate of the Galaxy Depends on Germans

"Our Germans are better than their Germans"
– The Right Stuff, 1983

Both Reptoids and Pleiadeans agree: The Fate of the Galaxy depends on Germans. Of course, there is a tendency to view one's own island, country, or planet, whichever it may be, as the center of the universe. The ancient Irish believed their island to be at the center of the universe. The ancient Hawaiians also believed their islands to be at the center of the world. Yet there is also a condition where a lot of foreign nations are coming to your place to exploit a natural resource, like in the Middle-East everyone goes to Iraq to fight over oil. Or like how everyone goes to Hawaii to fight over the best-priced hotels, the nicest spots on the beach, and the hottest Hawaiian women. So sometimes this self-centered view is at least partially true. *If* you have the metaphorical "Dune Spice" of the Universe.

In this case it is a peculiar fact that both Pleiadeans and Reptoids, who are at war with each other, **[27W] [A31]** are both incoherently obsessed with German People. Both as super-soldiers **[30Z] [26Z] [8H] [4D]** and as sex-partners. **[A32] [A33] [36G]** The Reptoids began harvesting and breeding Germans like Orks for use as Super-Soldiers since at least the 1920s. **[4D] [8H] [30Z] [3C] [A31]** This isn't just us Germans tooting our own horn here. (for the record I'm part Irish, English, American,

Italian, French, Austrian, Californian, Texan, Kekistani, Ginger, and German) This is a fact that other UFO researchers like Dr. Michael Salla have noticed as well. Pleiadean Women get themselves transferred to duties aboard the Starship Excelsior stationed near earth just so they can beam down and have sex with middle-aged men of German descent. [36G] [A32] [A33] The Reptoids based their whole first attempt at world-domination on Germans, by allying with Germans, backing the Germans, giving the Germans technology and crack and forging them into a proxy-army to try to take over the world. We remember this in history as the World War 2 period. Both before and after World War 2 on this Timeline, The Reptoids proceeded to forge German bloodlines into Super-Soldier Shock-Troops as intergalactic Storm-Troopers "Space-NAZIs" with which they are trying to take over the rest of the Galaxy right now. This all continues unabated to this very day and it's getting worse. [8H] [4D] [30Z] [3C] [A31] [A32] [A33] [36G]

The Galactic Federation of World's war against the Reptoid Empire is not going great. The Reptoid empire in combination with the Nacht Waffen German Super-Soldiers has pushed the Pleiadeans and the Galactic Federation of Worlds into a highly militant defensive mode as they struggle for survival against these violent enslaving existential threats. It's kind of like one of the bad Star-Trek timelines where the Klingons, Romulans, or Cardassians are winning the war and threatening to defeat and enslave the Federation, and then Captain Picard goes all evil and HAM and kicks their asses on the dark side mirror-universe again -kind of like that. In real life the Galactic Federation is starting to get desperate. Their mentors, the Andromedan-Ascended-Masters, predict for them defeat and falling underneath a Galactic Tyranny in 350 years time. Probably due to the combined activities of the Nacht-Waffen, Reptoids, and Zeta-Reticuli "Dark-Triad". This has brought the Galactic Federation of Worlds and the Pleiadeans back to square-one, what they believe to be both the source of their problems, and an opportunity for Salvation: Earth. [12L] [A31]

Of course they try not to give in to fear and try put a bold face on things, as Space Elves always do, to keep their vibes high, but the truth is things for them are going not well. Not well enough for the Pleiadeans to be looking to more Terran Super-Soldiers as a means for their salvation. There is a consistent pattern that the aggression, ruthlessness, and cunning of the Sikar-Reptoid-Orion Group has been besting them at every turn, on every planet, for many decades, if not centuries. **[12L] [A31]** So much so that they are turning towards the idea of arming Terrans, especially Americans (because we have it like that) and especially those of German descent, as front-line Shock Troops in their wars against the Reptoids and The Orion Group specifically to counter the Germans that the Reptoids have already armed and are using as front-line shock troops against them. So that they can say like in the movie *The Right Stuff* (1983), *"Our Germans are better than their Germans,"*. So you see the cooption of Earth by the Pleiadeans and the Galactic Federation of Worlds is not only altruistic in nature, but is based rather upon power-balance real-politics that the Galactic Federation of Worlds is trying to synergize along with their own codes of laws, ethics, spirituality, and The Prime Directive. **[12L] [A31]**

In their own histories and mythologies of hundreds of thousands of years ago, the Pleiadeans carry with them the memory of an ancient defeat at the hands of the Reptoids. [Kind of like JRR Tolkien's 2nd Age, except Sci-Fi and real-world] A defeat and enslavement so total, so complete, that the remnant of their race were only saved by the avenging fire of *'9th Dimensional Beings'*, probably what we would call the Holy Angels of God unleashed to save a remnant of their Space-Elf race. For them this represented a type of cosmic cataclysm for both their own people and the Sikar-Reptoids which they do not want to have to repeat.

Thus, the phenomenon of the Pleiadean Florence Nightingales beaming down to earth and having sex with middle-age men of German descent **[36G]** is in part due to a type of silent-desperation, an unspoken fear amongst some of the Pleiadean Women, an un-acknowledged undercurrent in Pleiadean society. Both a fear of dying childless AND the Galactic Federation of Worlds being conquered and enslaved by the Reptoids and The Orion Group. The woman on the street in their Federation can see that things are not working no matter what Commander

Thor-Han-Eredyon says in one of his public-relations releases. Kind of like how the Ukrainian people know they are slowly being defeated by the Russians, even as President Zelinski puts a happy smiley-face on things. Their battle-strategies are not working, the Federation I mean. Yet the race of men is similar enough to them in physiognomy and genetics, capable of love, and yet of a far more primitive, barbaric, violent, and ruthless deportment, kind of like *Tarzan of the Apes*. These women are deliberately defying the Prime Directive, and all standards of decency for any planet, on a kind of self-appointed secret mission. Because they believe their civilization needs more children with Terran and especially German-blood going into the future. In hopes of countering the violence, militancy, and cunning of the Reptoids as a long-term strategy. In a way it is the Pleiadean Women's hippie-style free-love counter to The Orion Empire's Nacht Waffen Super-Soldier program. These women hope to raise up children of mixed Pleiadean and German blood with enough *'Gott mit uns'* as part of their alliance to fight off The Orion Group threat. They believe they do so for the greater good. For the record they could probably just buy us a beer and ask nicely.

The Ontological Shock-Collar

*"I remember Wesley asking me a similar question when he was
little, and I tried desperately to give him an answer. But everything
I said sounded inadequate. Then I realized that scientists and
philosophers have been grappling with that question for centuries
without coming to any conclusion.... I think I'm saying that we
struggle all our lives to answer it, that it's the struggle that is
important. That's what helps us to define our place in the universe."*
*— Dr. Beverly Crusher, Star-Trek the Next Generation,
1987 to 1994*

Am I really just a Cosmic Space-Money? I have heard it postulated
that one of the reasons the Men-In-Black (MIB) decided not to go
public with Alien Disclosure in 1947 is the repercussions it might have for
the very fabric of our psyches, societies, religions, and The Church. What
if Jesus was an Alien? [A32] What if I'm really just a cosmic space-monkey? Or an ant in an Alien Ant-Farm? What if I'm really just an Amoeba
in some Alien's petri dish? Could I handle the truth?

We have to remember that as Jews, Christians, and Muslims, we have
the largest and most consistent group of Spirit-Walkers on earth. Enoch,
Isiah, Ezekiel, Jesus, John, Mohammad, Colton Burpo – peace be upon
them all, were all Spirit-Walkers that walked up the dimensional planes
to the heavenly realms, saw Almighty God on his throne and returned to
tell about it. Apostle John was punished for saying no-one had seen God
by a direct summons himself later as he attests in Apocalypse of John

chapter 4. We have to stick to our guns here. We have a long history with these Covenants and the Almighty God of the Universe who gave them. It may well be that the other star-nations have no such Covenants with The Great Architect of all creation. They might know as much about our Holy Covenants as the Anunnaki-Pagan Civilizations surrounding ancient Israel. Christianity grew up and ate the Roman Empire despite all odds. Islam grew up and ate everything else. These are successful, powerful Covenants that are greatly to be feared.

The Many Jesuses of the Alien Groups:

All of the different Extraterrestrial Groups with whom we are now in contact claim to be Jesus. The Pleiadeans claim to be Jesus. The Zeta-Reticuli Greys claim to be Jesus. **[18R]** The Anunnaki claim to be Jesus. **[43N]** **[40K]** The Reptoids claim to be Jesus. The New Age Ascended Masters of the Intergalactic Confederation of Worlds also claim to be Jesus. **[41L]** Apparently there's a lot of Jesus to go around. There are many differences between the various Alien Species and civilizations that we have catalogued over the last 100 years, but one thing remains the same: They all claim to be Jesus. This seems to be some type of cosmic-constant. The rule, rather than the exception. **[43N]** **[18R]** **[A32]** **[40K]** **[41L]** If we meet a new Alien species, maybe say some type of Sentient Jello-creature with eyes-on-stalks, many things about them may be different from other Alien Species, but we can be fairly certain that they too will claim to be Jesus.

Are they just trying to scramble our brains? Are they trying to out-crazy me with an A-causality Superpower like Bug's Bunny? -It's because all the different Aliens don't always talk to one-another. It is a case of the hand not talking to the foot. It is a case of one group of Aliens not talking to the other groups of Aliens to get their story straight. It would have been better if one group of Aliens pretended to be Jesus and another group of Aliens pretended to be Buddha, and another group of Aliens pretended to be Mohammad etc.. But they got greedy. They flew too close to the sun. They fumbled the football. Bit off more than they can chew. Screwed the pooch on this one. But they do all examine our cultural anthropology scientifically to identify the cultural figures who have the greatest impact on our conscious and subconscious minds. It is a form of low-effort mind-control attempted from a scientifically advanced civilization attempting to prey upon a developing civilization like ours. It's kind of like when your mom and dad dress up in Easter-Bunny outfits and tell you they're the Easter-bunny, or when one of them dresses up as Santa Claus and the other dresses up as his Elf-helper and they really try to convince you that they're Santa-Clause and his First-Elf. I mean, I dunno what went on at your house.

To the first accusation I think we should tell the Aliens that *they* are *our* cosmic-space-monkeys; They are like Crow-Magnon-Man in comparison to us. We're the new-and-improved-model, after all, any way you slice it. They're cold-product, a relic from the past, like Brittany-Spears' portfolio from the 1990s. And if they try to probe us, *we'll* probe *them* ten times more. -Take that, Aliens.

From all the available evidence so far from various Contactees, Reptoids, Pleiadeans, Anunnaki, Mormons, - we all have unreconcilable religious differences even after thousands of years of arguing about it, which I think is a good thing. It means that we can and should still argue about religion even in the Space-Age, and fight giant civilization-ending wars over it, and Nuke each-other because of it, potentially for hundreds of thousands of years into the future, just as long as we like, . . . maybe forever. Anyone telling you the argument on religion is closed in 2024 is probably a Cone-Head, a hippie peace-creep, or giant talking-Iguana in a Henry Kissinger suit.

The Many Cosmologies of the Pleiadean Peoples and The Galactic Federation of Worlds

"I find your lack of faith disturbing. . ."
– Darth Vader to the Imperial Council, Star Wars Episode 4

God's Debris

At one extreme end of their religious theologies some of them entertain the 'God's Debris Theory', this is the side of their religious ideas that is the closest to Atheism, although it is not (quite) Atheism – that is, according to them, at one time there was an original, personal, and sovereign God who created and ruled over many universes. However, in testing the limits of what he/she/they/it could accomplish, God contemplated that the only thing it might not be able to do is cease to exist. (this reveals a type of death-wish some of them have towards the actual Cosmic Creator) Finally, after billions of Aeons of attempting everything eventually resulting in infinite boredom -God decided to attempt the undoable, therefor trying their hand at true omnipotence -and willed itself to die. Supposedly, the result of this was a fragmentation into an infinite number of seeder souls – the children of God or infinite and sentient energy beings which became us and all sentient and non-sentient life, matter, and energy. This theory holds that gradually over time, billions of years, the fragmented souls (us) that were at one time God slowly, and through processes such as gay-marriage merge back together in an infinite process that will one day result in the re-unification and re-birth of God as one sentient singular consciousness in an eternal cycle. This is the way amongst their religious or cosmological ideas that is nearest (but not quite) Atheism, as it holds that God at one time did, but does not now (exactly), but one day will again -exist. This cosmology is not true, especially now, Almighty God is alive and well and in control and the judge of all multiverses.

The Egg Theory

In the middle of their cosmologies some of them entertain the 'Egg Theory' – that is the idea that there is in reality only one unique consciousness who/it created the universes and now spends and infinite amount of time incarnating individually through the eyes of each character, person, and animal lives. In this theory all such separations are actually an illusion -I am you and you are me, and we/I is passing through an infinitely long experiment of artificially infinite and illusory avatars in an attempt to not feel lonely. This cosmology is not true, as both I and you will be individually judged for our actions, thoughts, and the results of our deeds by the actual Eternal God who is not us, in a way that is perfectly just and (hopefully) seasoned with a bit of grace from the actual Mercy-Seat of the only One God of the highest heavens.

The Cosmic Consciousness

Coming nearer to actual Monotheism, some of them understand the Higher-Power-Divine-Cosmic-Creator as having a separate, omniscient, eternal, and sovereign will; of which the actual, tangible, and inevitable Cosmic Law (Natural Law) is an extension of this person. Nevertheless, they still tend to refer to the Cosmic Creator as she/her or they/it -misgendering him I suppose. This cosmology is slightly astray as the real Cosmic Creator is firmly (perhaps infinitely) masculine energy as a dynamic creative force, sovereign, father-like, patriarchal in nature, no matter how much the disbelievers may hate it. He is to be feared and revered and was is and shall be sovereign now and always and deserves all the honor both for the creation of the universes we inhabit and for we ourselves and all his benefits to us.

The Tyrannical Architect

Some of them are actual prodigal-monotheists in the sense that they really know that the Cosmic Creator is omnipotent, omniscient, masculine, patriarchal, the judge of all universes and planes and their inhabitants, and father-like in nature, HOWEVER, they defiantly disagree with some aspects of the way God is running things, maybe somewhat like prophet Job. A good illustration of this perspective came out of the Matrix-series, where Neo goes to meet The Architect. In this depiction Neo finds a secret key to unlock a door where he is engulfed in an overpowering blinding white light and finds himself standing in the presence of The Architect. We immediately see that The Architect also has his eye (or perfect knowledge) on an infinite number of other "Neos" -souls within his creation. The Architect is clearly meant to represent God in this illustration as he is depicted in the classical caricature of God as an old white man with a white beard seated at perfect repose and authority in an immaculate white suit. He already knows what Neo is thinking and the questions he has and what he will ask before he asks them, and The Architect is able to explain to Neo about the nature of his creation in which Neo and his friends live. The Architect explains to Neo that he, The Architect, is going to destroy the entire Matrix along with all of its denizens (somewhat like God destroying the world during Noah's flood) and that Neo is given the option of selecting 24 survivors that will repopulate the earth (somewhat like Noah, or like when God threatened to wipeout the Hebrews and start again with Moses only) Neo must go along with the program or be exterminated along with them as well, but he has the choice to go along with it willingly or to defy it. If Neo submits to The Architect's program Neo will serve the function of returning the 'program' back to its original form. (Like prophet Noah returned the religion or the 'program' of the world back to perfect monotheism, the rest of the rebels being exterminated) The Architect has already explained that Neo and the others souls always retain Free Will; Neo can choose to obey the Architect's program, which will result in this small remnant seeder-group (like prophet Noah & family) and the rest being exterminated, or to disobey the Architect entirely, go back to his rebel-friends, and they all will be exterminated together, BUT Neo will have kept faith with his friends till death, dying with them, but defying The Architect's designs. In this depiction God/ The Architect is portrayed as a cold and calculating tyrant, or maybe even a psychopath, who unfortunately holds near-omnipotent power over The Matrix/World and its denizen souls, except for the fact that those souls retain Free-Will. At the last they may all choose to perish together, keeping faith with each other till death, in defiance of The Architect's will; even though they know The Architect will remain and create another Matrix/World/Universe after their world is destroyed. In the third film we find out that a peace-settlement has been brokered by The Oracle (A Mother-Mary or Jesus figure?) between the souls in The Matrix and The Architect, to stay his hand of judgement for yet awhile longer to allow the souls in the Matrix to continue to live on in relative peace, at least for a time. In this depiction, Neo as the hero of the film remains defiant against The Architect/God and will not bend the knee to his tyrannical will, even though The Architect seems to be near-omnipotent, Neo holds out the hope that some alternative better way forward may be found that doesn't involve submitting to The Architect's will. This is essentially the deportment or outlook of some of the Pleiadeans and the Andromedin Ascended Masters whom they look up to: they view God as an eternal tyrant, and the best they can do is a kind of brokered peace-deal with him that will allow them to continue to live out their incarnations in relative peace for awhile. This attitude stems from the fact that many souls within the creation do not agree with some aspects of the way God is running things, be it hell, sin, evil, the problem of pain or whathave you, even though they want to keep faith with one-another. That is why the Galactic Federation of World's definition of justice is *transforming pain into peace.* **[A31]** For them, *pain* in all its forms is the enemy, while *peace* their ultimate goal, having long ago rejected God's sovereign criteria of Right and Wrong, Good and Evil, they have rather come up with their own agreed-upon morality by mutual-consent and by popular demand. That's why the dream of this type of soul -the ultimate honor, is in their imagination, like Neo with The Architect, for all souls with Free Will to unite in common-cause together against the Omnipotent Architect on behalf of each-other, and to show him their defiance in mutual-solidarity as did the people of Noah.

These are the basic Cosmologies of the Pleiadeans, the Galactic-Federation-of-Worlds peoples, and the Andromedin New Age Ascended Masters of the middle-planes whom the Pleiadeans admire. They consider themselves to be peoples of the twilight **[12L] [A31]** ; neither of the darkness in its rapacious vampirism, like the Reptoids and Greys, nor of God's blinding light from the higher planes with the Holy Angels which they view to be too judgmental, restrictive, and fascist. Particularly disagreeing with the patriarchal sovereign and absolutist nature of God, and the forced puritanical holiness of the higher realms from which they have fallen.

Andromedan New Age Ascended Masters Smoke the Peace-Pipe: Welcome to the Multiverse

"The dark side clouds everything. Impossible to see the future is."
— *Yoda, Star Wars Episode 3*

It is impossible to talk about Aliens without talking about religion, because like holes in the ground, they have a lot of different opinions on it. This is a complicated subject due to the peoples of the twilight. The Pleiadeans and the Intergalactic Confederation New Age Ascended Master people who claim to be 'in the middle' of the dimensional planes. They admit that they are not the highest. [12L] They try to be honest about things they know can and will soon be verified as a point of wisdom. But they have a warped middle-dimensional perspective. They certainly know that there are higher 'brighter' dimensions above them, but they do not agree with the higher heavenly realms deeming them something like extremist-light-siders, their viewpoint on the holy angels of God and the higher companions. They essentially view the upper realms above them to be something like divine-fascists. Thus, in their own perspective they seek to maintain the 'balance' between the light and the dark sides. [12L] This is where you get a lot of the 'balance' references in the New Age religions, Buddhism, Taoism, Hinduism, and in Star Wars. Again, the analogy of Neo acting in defiance of The Architect is apropos here. These 'twilight-beings' are not with God because there are aspects of the way God is running things they do not agree with. Nevertheless, they desire to maintain solidarity with each other. Of course, the New Age Ascended Masters of the Intergalactic Confederation also claim to be Jesus along with all the other Extraterrestrial groups.

The New Age Ascended Master peoples of the Intergalactic Confederation of Worlds are at a higher dimensional state, [12L] kind of like some of your teachers in High School, and are in a good position to talk down at us. However, that does not mean they are right about everything. It's kind of like how you grew up after high school and now realize how limited your High School teachers were - but at the time they were in a good position to talk down to you and moralize at you about responsibility. At the time you weren't quite sure if you should be sassing them, or asking them hard-questions or not. But it turns out later that their knowledge and perspective was limited and a lot of the hard questions you asked of them were totally valid and they didn't know how to answer very well, and overall they just had a small, sad, ghay perspective - kind of like that. This is going to be the next 1,000 years on earth with the New Age Ascended Master Intergalactic Confederation people moralizing at us like this just like all your teachers in Grade school, Jr. High, and High-school. Just like your 2nd Grade teacher didn't like guns.

The New Age Ascended Master Peoples and Intergalactic Confederation of Worlds Peoples don't agree with the way God is running things. Kind of like Neo in the Matrix-series is defiant against The Architect. They dream of a day when all the created-souls of the multiverses will join hands in a big circle, singing Cum-by-Ya, as a mutual-act of peaceful defiance against the Great Immortal Tyrant. These are the basic facts that they are concealing, and about which they have carefully-constructed counter-narratives to try and avoid talking about. This has to do with what they conceal, and what they reveal. That's why they talk the way they do, like the Tortoise from Kung-Fu Panda, because they are trying to circle you up to their dimensional planes 'in the middle' by their own admission, 'maintaining balance' without allowing you to escape into the higher RIGHTEOUS AEON planes with Almighty God to which the Holy Covenants call us.

They have a perspective kind of like your grandmother. She doesn't like pain. She doesn't want you to be in pain either. She also conceals a lot of secrets about her misspent youth from way before you were born that she will try to never let get out. She is not going to bald-face lie if she can help it. But she will omit. She will talk-around, change the subject, deflect, and intentionally not-remember certain things. She will craft a narrative for you that she genuinely believes is in your (and hers) best-interest. It will leave out certain details, and accentuate others, whatever is favorable to her cause. She would prefer you move-in across the street and get a nice comfy job with a wifey and 2.5 kids and come over every day to her place and eat Quiche.

As a young man of 18 I spent a summer with a Jedi who would become one of planet-earth's greatest and most well-known New-Age Gurus. He has become much more famous since then. I want to say he had at least five full-time disciples at the time and they all wore leather sandals and man-dresses like Jesus. They wanted to train me as a disciple. They were charmed by my piano musical compositional abilities - maybe somewhat like king Saul was charmed by David's harp. Something like Jesus and his first-century disciples we traveled from house-to house and slept on futon-mattresses. They were vegetarians. They taught meditation and breathing-exercises and a host of other light-and-love spiritual-philosophies centered on the love ethic. Yet I was rudely awakened one morning off my futon-mattress to hear our Master Guru shouting violently into the phone. Apparently, a seminar-attendee did not want to pay the full price; apparently these seminars were quite costly; several thousand dollar a pop I think and back then that used to be a lot of money. You know when there is an argument that is really sharp and unpleasant and has what the New-Agers might call 'negative-energy'. It had negative energy. Our Guru seemed almost caught in a sin to see me standing there, awoken off my futon-mattress, as if he had forgotten that I was still in the house. All the other disciples and householders were elsewhere . . . hugging it out or something. He seemed to do some quick back-peddling after hanging up the phone: 'it's for them' he said, 'I had so-and-so from last year sell all the furniture in his house to pay . . .' It was an interesting exposition of the inner-man in an unguarded moment. I wonder if God or Destiny had placed me here? It was an ugly moment, and ran counter to the public-face of the man and the organization. It's hard to maintain an ever-light-and-love public persona, it's not realistic. In our situation now I wonder how long the Pleiadeans and/or Andromedin New Age Ascended Masters will be able to maintain an ever-light-and-love public persona. It's hard to maintain. People have failings. People have rough-edges. People have ugly-moments. People need Jesus. For me it was ugly enough and incongruous enough and petty enough to move on from, I phoned my military-recruiter and he came to pick me up, and delivered me more-or-less directly to boot camp.

Conceptual Model of Dimensional Planes

Dimensional Plane - God

Dimensional Plane - Michael, Gabriel, Angel of Death

Dimensional Plane - 24 Biblical Eldars

Dimensional Plane - Biblical saints that made it, my godfather Paul, Abraham etc.

Dimensional Plane -

Dimensional Plane -

Dimensional Plane - 24 New Age Ascended Master Eldars, this is probably an imitation of Biblical 24 Eldars in a 'middle-plane',

Dimensional Plane - New Age 'Ascended Masters' Intergalactic Confederation somewhere here

(ignore God because they don't agree with him)

Dimensional Plane -

Dimensional Plane -

Dimensional Plane - **However, we also have Light-Bodies that simultaneously exist here, it's complicated**

Pleiadeans also have Light-Bodies that simultaneously exist here

Dimensional Plane - Pleiadeans

(also ignore God because they don't agree with him)

Dimensional Plane - Terrans / **Me & you right now** / Draconians / Reptoids / Greys / Sometimes Pleiadeans

Dimensional Plane - Draconians / Reptoids / Greys / some of these guys try to get up one dimension

Dimensional Plane - Draconians / Reptoids / Greys / Dante's circles of hell

Dimensional Plane - worse entities and worse dimensions / Dante's circles of hell

Dimensional Plane - worse entities and worse dimensions / Dante's circles of hell

Dimensional Plane - worse entities and worse dimensions / Dante's circles of hell

Dimensional Plane - worse entities and worse dimensions / Dante's circles of hell

Dimensional Plane - worse entities and worse dimensions / Dante's circles of hell

I Patiently Explain to the Pleiadeans Their True Spiritual History and Origins Most of Which They Have Forgotten

Once upon a day of eternity, a group of angels in heaven (New Age/ Pleiadean speak: '9th -Dimensional Light-Beings') gathered to discuss the suffering of some of their brothers and sisters who had been justly judged unto the hell-worlds for some sins they had committed. They knew that their friends and brethren suffered for some sins they had committed, yet like innocent babes, they knew not what was suffering -nor what was sin. For there is no sin, nor suffering in heaven. In this way their hands were numb. Nevertheless, as beings of love and compassion they were curious about this suffering and about this sin as they did contemplate (and gaze upon) their brethren. In this contemplation they (jointly) decided that they would pray unto the Almighty God that He might grant a reprieve unto some of these. Yet as no affirmation of their prayer was accepted in the hour they so desired -they did decide to meet at regular intervals in what we might call a 'prayer-vigil' for this is how they began their journey. I too will keep your vigil with you, although I am a Christian. Alas, the Almighty God did not harken unto their prayer in the hour they so desired! And yet their hands were numb. Nevertheless, the spirit of persistence was in them, -although their hands were numb, and so they became like a group, enjoying the camaraderie of one-another, still meeting at regular intervals -it became a sect or religion amongst the angels unto itself -and yet their hands were numb. Within this group rose up a spirit of defiance: *'we shall never cease our vigil until every last one of our brethren are redeemed, -neither shall they be forgotten'* As we might remember a Prisoner-of-War, and as they looked down, yet their hands were numb. But this redemption was not in the ability of the angels, nor the purpose for which they had been created, straying slightly. Persisting thus . . . at length a calamity occurred and being all of one-accord they said unto The Lord God Almighty, *'we do hold some of your judgements, O God, to be in error'* -thinking only of the suffering of the hell-beings whom God had (intentionally) forgotten. At this they lost their first estate, and as this was in a time before Michael, Almighty God dispatched the foremost and most luminous of all his Archangels to banish the rebels; the Archangel who was most prominent in the time before Michael. Thus, they view these two in the same light -Almighty God and his foremost Archangel in the time before Michael. For it was he -the Archangel before Michael, who seized them sternly by orders from on high -to hurl them one and all of the rebel group unto the lower-planes. Those who had gazed too intently upon the suffering of those the Lord-God had (intentionally) forgotten. This is the origins of the Eldar Race in the physical planes. And there they sat (in 3rd-dimensional space, the World, the Matrix) looking at one-another. They had been granted a reprieve from The Lord-God, however, and found themselves in the middle-planes, as their deeds deserved. For they had raised the 2nd commandment 'love thy neighbor' above the 1st 'thou shalt love the Lord Your God with all your heart, mind and strength'. They had been separated from The Lord-God, as prodigal-angels, due to this error. Because they sought to judge the Lord-God in his creation (Like prophet Job) and some of its aspects -debating about what they knew-not.

Once again they were apt to make rules by mutual-consent. Looking at each-other they decided upon several axioms: #1 Never would they repent of the compassion for others -even the hell-beings, for which they had fallen from grace #2 As for God? They would not speak of him, as when a child is angry with his parent, and try to put him out-of-mind, for he had been an abusive, tyrannical parent in their estimation, both for the Hell-beings and for their own treatment. Yet part of their prayer had been answered for, their hands were no longer numb, sharing in the sufferings of the sinners.

Later, the day came when God made man in his own image, and most of the Angels bowed low to him and to Adam, yet the prodigal-angels were absent for the purpose for which they had been created -to assist man during the period of his spiritual development and as eternal servants, friends, and lovers; for this rebel group had become prodigals, sojourning in the middle-planes. The Archangel, however, refused to bow to Adam, saying 'I will not serve him, -not him who will shed blood and work iniquity, but only The Most Gracious (God)'. Thus a separate controversy began with the Archangel who chose to both envy (for his Destiny) and hate Adam. Another group of angels followed the Archangel hating both God, man, and themselves. But the Archangel hated only man. (breach of the 2nd Commandment, but retaining the 1st, and the 3rd)

The prodigal angels, whose hands were no longer numb, never repented of the purpose for which they had been created, although they had gotten side-tracked by the hell-beings, gazing too intently, they were impatient for God's Grace, but neither were they too proud to lift up those who had fallen low, -they had been granted a reprieve.

Thus some the prodigal angels (the Eldar Race) seek to fulfill the original purpose for which they had been created, being the caretakers of man during the period of his spiritual development, even though they are side-tracked and sojourning in the middle-planes. (for many hundreds of thousands of years)

Even though the prodigal angels had been impatient, seeking God's Grace on behalf of the Hell-beings, and fell from Grace thereby, -The Most Gracious God did hear their prayer, and the prayers of others, sending an incarnation of his Word in his own time, season, and place to Holy Terra to bring forth some of the prisoners out of the lower-planes. < Thus you may explain Christianity to the Elder-races, and some of them will choose to understand.

Anunnaki Intervention in the Middle-East: Greater Joshua and Greater David in a Galaxy of Giants

"And there we saw the Nephilim, the sons of Anak, which come of the Nephilim: and we were in our own sight as grasshoppers, and so we were in their sight."

— Book of Numbers 13:33 ERV

We now know that many of the demi-gods of the ancient world were probably spacemen. There was a large amount of interference from the Anunnaki star-nations throughout the middle-east stretching back for thousands of years in the ancient world. **[43N] [7G] [28X]** They brought a lot of Alien technology and knowledge to earth in the ancient world and were therefor revered as gods come down out of the heavens in Egypt, Sumer, Babylon and elsewhere. There is archeological evidence showing the early Pharoahs of Egypt with elongated skulls - indicative of mixed human and Anunnaki blood. Some of the early crowns of the Egyptian kings were probably made in a deliberate attempt to accentuate or simulate an elongated-skull, as this phenotype of the Anunnaki bloodline had come to be seen as a sign of royalty and/or demigodhood. Although the percentage % of actual Anunnaki star-nation blood in the bloodline of the Egyptian Pharoahs had become extremely diluted by the time of Moses, we see that the office of the Pharoah still carried on in the presumption of its ancestors -holding the Pharoah out to be a god. Centuries previous to this father Abraham had similar experiences with king Nimrod of Sumer who had also claimed to be a god. The king of Sumer was probably also of mixed human/Anunnaki star-nation blood. Previous to king Nimrod, king Gilgamesh of Sumer had probably been of mixed human/Anunnaki blood, a *Gibboreem* (a mutant). Our Transcendent Omni-Omni God spent a lot of time with the children of Israel in the Old Testament disabusing them of the idea of the divinity of any of these lesser so-called 'gods', and proving dominance over all the lesser gods of the nations over thousands of years. Our Muslim brothers are also in agreement with us on this matter, recounting for us both the story of the presumption of Pharoah and the story of father Abraham vs. king Nimrod.

Walking down the centuries the Phoenician-Philistine peoples were also of mixed Anunnaki and human blood. This gave rise to the race of giants Joshua and Caleb found living in the Promised Land. **[28X]** Despite the conquests of Joshuah and the Hebrew Judges, the Philistine-Anunnaki bloodlines were still existent in the Lavant 500 years later by the time of David at about 1,000 BC. Although these Anunnaki bloodlines were both diluted over time due to intermarriage, and intentionally hunted to near-extinction by Zionist zealots like Joshua, Sampson, and David, -there was still at least a little bit of Syrophoenician blood left on the earth by the time of Christ to make its appearance in the Syrophoenician woman of Matthew 15. Which is also part of the reason why Christ replies to her, "It is not right to take the children's bread and toss it to the dogs."

The Jews, Christians, and Muslims on this planet in 2024 have to realize that we are being tested with the likeness of what our ancestors were tested with. Abraham and Moses both repudiated the demigodhood of the Anunnaki kings. Joshua and David hunted the Anunnaki bloodlines to near-extinction. **[28X]** If this star-nation with high hubris wants to return to the 3rd rock from the sun for any reason it should be with high trepidation. The sons of Abraham have multiplied on the earth, to whom Almighty God also spoke, *"Look now toward heaven, and tell the stars, if thou be able to number them: So shall your descendants be."* [Genesis 15:15]

Holy Terra

"For the earth shall be filled with the knowledge of the glory of the LORD, as the waters cover the sea."
– Habakkuk 2:14 KJB

Almighty God has seeded Holy Terra with a plethora of prophetic Covenants, a situation that is probably somewhat rare throughout the Cosmos, especially on this plane. The most prominent of these on this planet at the moment are Judaism, Christianity, and Islam. But the Zoroastrians, Druze, the original Vedic Brahmans, Sikhs, Bahais, and those of the ancient order of Melchizedek have or had similar Covenants with God also. Prophet Enoch, prophet Noah, and prophet Abraham had small followings during their lifetimes which may be considered pre-Judaic, the legacies of which have nevertheless been culminated forward within the traditions of modern Judaism, Christianity, and Islam, with each and all claiming the former prophets as their own at the Culmination of Time. That is, each of these prophets and Covenants has or had a relationship with the One, Almighty, Omniscient, Creator-God of the universe; not to be confused with lesser deities, angels, demons, space-men, or demigods. I call these culminated monotheistic religions of Holy Terra, "Universal" for they are all covenants and schools of thought given to mankind designed to lead the soul into relationship with God. Not equal are Buddhism and Hinduism amongst them, for these are Pantheistic religions which deny the personhood and sovereignty of God, as do the Pleiadeans and the Andromedins.

Christianity and Islam have never had a bad year. That is, since their inception 2,000 and 1,400 years ago respectively on Holy Terra, there have always been more converts in each successive year for each of them than the year before. Like owning two stocks that only ever go up in value. This phenomenon is remarkable in the history of the world, and may seem miraculous. From the Pleiadean and Andromedin point of view it is a major terror. These religions are overly-healthy in their view, judgmental, evangelistic, militaristic, warlike, patriarchal, sufficiently organized and decentralized to present a major problem going forward in time. The Pleiadeans have to attempt to seduce the greatest portion of Christians and Muslims on earth to their philosophical aims, hopefully in their view, coopting both religions whole and prevaricating them into their Pantheist religion-type (that they will claim is not a religion). This is probably not going to happen for the most part, as the greater portion of 2 Billion Christians, and 2 Billion more Muslims on earth will probably never downgrade their knowledge of a patriarchal, personal, singular, Almighty, sovereign, creator-God into a feeling. Yet they must try, for these two dogmatic religions especially threaten the Pleiadeans and the Galactic Federation of World's carefully-laid plans for the Galaxy. And they fear the Cosmic Crusaders which shall inevitably be part of this Galaxy's history very soon. I don't blame them. I would fear us too. But perhaps they may take comfort in the fact that Christianity and Islam in their true forms take aim also at the demonic Sikhar for eradication. We shall loose the bands of Orion. For which I hope much common-cause between us and them may be made. Also I believe that mankind with our large evangelical prophetic covenants will serve as a vehicle and an opportunity for the Pantheistic Pleiadeans and others to reconcile with the Cosmic Creator and regain their first estate in the heavenly Planes.

Until then the Pleiadeans and Andromedins are hell-bent on conflating the Prophetic Covenants of Holy Terra with the worship of Enki, Enlil, or some other Anunnaki Cone-Head which the Jews Christians and Muslims specifically deny by name. Some of them do this in full-knowledge of their error. The only appropriate response to this is for the Jews, Christians, and

Muslims on this planet to intentionally and wrongfully conflate the Pleiadean and Andromedin rebellion with the Luciferian Rebellion. They are in actuality at least 2 or 3 different rebellions of angels against God, kicked down to the lower middle-planes that are now the Pleiadean and Andromedin peoples, but it is just in this case to wrongfully conflate them all as being part-and-parcel with the Luciferian Rebellion, as they also wrongfully conflate our Holy Covenants with the worship of Ancient Astronauts. The general population of Evangelicals on this planet (and probably also the Muslims) are going to wrongfully conflate the Pleiadean-Andromedin faction with the Luciferian faction. I am not going to disabuse them of this misunderstanding as long at the Pleiadean-Andromedin faction also wants to wrongfully conflate the Holy Covenants of Terra with Sikhar agreements or the worship of Cone-heads.

Those of them who claim our monotheistic covenants to be on par with Ba'al worship and the paganism of a thousand lesser tribes are woefully mistaken. The Jews, Christians, and Muslims specifically disavow Ba'al worship and have from the beginning. Specifically disavow Anunnaki-worship as was practiced by the worshippers of Gilgamesh, Nimrod, and Pharoah, and have from the beginning. As Jews, Christians, and Muslims we have the lion's-share of spirit-walkers on this planet with prophets Enoch, Ezekial, Jesus, Mohammad (during the journey by night) and the Apostle John amongst many others traveling up the Astral planes to the very throne-room of Almighty God and returning yet again to tell the tale. Apostle John, who had inaccurately claimed no-one had seen God, was later punished for his error with his own terrifying Revelation: [Apocalypse of John 4:1-11]

1After this I looked and saw a door standing open in heaven. And the voice I had previously heard speak to me like a trumpet was saying, "Come up here, and I will show you what must happen after these things."

2At once I was in the Spirit, [spirit-walker] *and I saw a throne standing in heaven, with someone seated on it. 3The One seated there looked like*

*jasper and carnelian, and a rainbow that gleamed like an emerald encir-
cled the throne. 4Surrounding the throne were twenty-four other thrones,
and on these thrones sat twenty-four elders dressed in white, with golden
crowns on their heads.*

*5From the throne came flashes of lightning, and rumblings, and peals of
thunder. Before the throne burned seven torches of fire. These are the seven
Spirits of God. 6And before the throne was something like a sea of glass,
as clear as crystal. In the center, around the throne, were four living creatures, covered with eyes in front and back. 7The first living creature was
like a lion, the second like a calf, the third had a face like a man, and the
fourth was like an eagle in flight. 8And each of the four living creatures
had six wings and was covered with eyes all around and within. Day and
night they never stop saying:*

*"Holy, Holy, Holy,
is the Lord God Almighty,
who was and is and is to come!"*

*9And whenever the living creatures give glory, honor, and thanks to the
One seated on the throne who lives forever and ever, 10the twenty-four
elders fall down before the One seated on the throne, and they worship
Him who lives forever and ever. They cast their crowns before the throne,
saying:*

*11 "Worthy are You, our Lord and God,
to receive glory and honor and power,
for You created all things;
by Your will they exist and came to be."*

It should be remembered amongst us that it is the Jews, Christians,
and Muslim who have the lion's share of prophets, seers, and spirit-walkers on this planet and that we jointly attest to the one, singular, masculine, patriarchal, omnipotent and omniscient Almighty-God of all the

universes, and that we are in Covenant with him. This is not within the experience of the Pleiadeans or Andromedins for many days as they are prodigal angels, and they have an incredible oversight in this regard, but in time the truth of all these matters shall be demonstrated yet again, in a greater cycle, just as with the prophets of old.

The Pleiadeans have a grotesque oversight in the matter, for they fail to realize or understand the Covenants from Almighty God that we on this planet have been covenanted with. All of us on planet earth are at least responsible for the legacy of prophet Noah, for most of us are descended of him, even if our family lines have not contracted any more recent covenant (of Judaism, Christianity, or Islam). This means that we are at least responsible for the Noahide Law, the first commandment of which is, "Do not deny God". It would be like if a door-to-door salesman came to your house to tell you that your family doesn't have to pay their mortgage, because the salesman doesn't have one and knows by experiential knowledge that not paying a mortgage has never resulted in penalties before. But your family still has to pay its mortgage, because your family made an agreement with the bank to pay a certain amount each month. Thus the Pleiadeans, not understanding any of this, labor on blissfully ignorant that those of you who they tempt away from your religion are in grave danger of being damned, because your ancestors made agreements with God that he expects to be upheld by bloodline and in perpetuity forever. *"6 These commandments that I give you today are to be on your hearts. 7 Impress them on your children. Talk about them when you sit at home and when you walk along the road, when you lie down and when you get up. 8 Tie them as symbols on your hands and bind them on your foreheads. 9 Write them on the doorframes of your houses and on your gates."* [Deuteronomy 6:6-9 NIV] This is because Almighty God intends to make of the whole Earth eventually *"a kingdom of priests and a holy nation."* [Exodus 19:6 NIV] in a greater way even than the Hebrews were a priestly people, a light to the nations. And again, *"For the earth will be filled with the knowledge of the glory of the LORD as the waters cover the sea."* [Habakkuk 2:14 NIV] . . . Our situation is not the same as theirs. It may well be that that

Pleiadeans re-incarnate throughout this plane more-or-less in perpetuity due to the situation and history of their souls. But their situation is not the same as ours. You should have known that your family's Covenant with God was more important to be upheld than accepting the sophistries of a foreign people. This situation is especially insidious because most of the Pleiadeans probably genuinely believe they work for the benefit of and the betterment of mankind, yet they have no understanding regarding the covenants our family lines have been covenanted with, and they lack the knowledge, ignore, or choose to forget, the personhood, patriarchy, and sovereignty of the real Cosmic Creator. Thus, the "sweet influences" of the Pleiades shall serve as a temptation and test for you and I and those of mankind who shall come after us.

Or maybe to put it in a way Pleiadeans might be able to understand: Pleiadeans do not understand Terran incarnation cycles. Some of the Jews, Christians, Muslims, and a handful of others graduate to much higher Planes (heavens). While the vast majority of Terrans fall down and are confined within the lower Planes (Hells) due to their hatred, greed, covetousness, lust, and the other deadly sins and that they forsook the Covenants that God had contracted with their ancestors.

Or let's look at it another way, Pleiadeans. This might resonate with you: Let's imagine that you are trying to be doctors or veterinarians of a thousand different species around the Galaxy. You know that each species will have its own needs as to its appropriate care. A fish species will need to live in a certain type of water, a mammal with five hearts will need a particular kind of care. If improper care is administered to the wrong species in can be very harmful, perhaps even resulting in physical death. Likewise, if you are able to tempt the Covenanted Terran away from his religion, this too may result in soul-death. This understanding of improper spiritual care needs to be communicated to the Pleiadeans, who will otherwise, and with every good and blissfully ignorant intention, tempt the Terran away from his Holy Covenants, which in many cases can be completely fatal. Furthermore, the actual, personal, one, singular, patriarchal, Almighty God of the Universe (who they either have forgotten or ignore) would probably credit such soul-deaths to the ledger of the Pleiadeans involved, resulting in what they would call bad Karma. Pleiadeans might actually be able to understand the necessity of all this. But they have an incredible blind-spot when it comes to the actual, one, singular, personal, masculine, patriarchal, creator-God of all the universe who they have either forgotten, are putting out of mind, or intentionally ignore.

Anunnaki Cone-Head Death-Star

The Anunnaki are an extremely scientifically advanced Alien group [43N] [A31] [12L] capable of building moon-sized Worldships, kind of like a star-wars Death Star. In the past, astronomical sightings of this technological terror throughout our solar-system have been called 'Planet X' or 'the Planet Nibiru'. In their natural state the Anunnaki have stupid-looking cone-heads. To overcompensate for this, most of the time they choose to create and inhabit giant artificially-grown avatars to walk around in on a given planet with superior styoil. Kind of like the giant blue avatar bodies from the movie 'Avatar' to overcompensate for their innate physical and psychological insecurities and their stupid-looking heads. In the ancient world on earth they created a lot of Anunnaki-human hybrids (also with cone-heads). As a matter of fact, a lot of the human royalty on earth back then who didn't have natural cone-heads would sometimes bind their children's normal-heads with compressed planks of wood in order to give them cone-heads (and probably also a splitting headache) over time as the baby's soft skulls were to develop. This is kind of like when you wore a mohawk hairstyle in highschool because all these other cool punk-rockers were doing it, but now you think back and ask yourself the question: 'what the heck was I thinking?' There were Anunnaki-human hybrids back then who became the people-groups we now call Phoenicians and/or Philistines, as is recorded in many of the ancient Babylonian and Sumerian texts, and in the Bible. [28X] As in, *"And there we saw the giants, the sons of Anak, which come of the giants: and we were in our own sight as grasshoppers, and so we were in their sight."* [**Numbers 13:33 KJV**] Goliath and the 6-fingered Giants in the land Joshua and Caleb killed were actually Anunnaki-human hybrids with cone-heads.

Despite their stupid-looking heads, the princes of the Anunnaki claim to be God. [**43N**] They claim to be the God of the Bible and are really emphatic about it. [**43N**] They said they give life and cause death. They said there is no such thing as any real higher Cosmic Creator above them. They said they are the top of the pyramid and they can prove it. They said they are the God of the Torah, Gospel, and Koran and there is no God or gods above them. They said that there is no such thing as a Cosmic Creator God other than them, and that the Jews, Christians, and Muslims who think that they may have Covenants with such a God are gravely mistaken. They said that Almighty God of the Universe does not exist, and even if he did exist, his hands are tied up to his neck and he is unable to do anything either good or bad. That's what they said. I'm just repeating what they said. They said that they would be happy to prove that there is no God, Cosmic-Creator, Super-Soul, or Great Architect above them. They said they can prove to the Jews, Christians, and Muslims on earth that they are the God of the Bible and the Koran as in Enki and Enlil and that nothing will stop them from proving it. [**43N**] They said they are the Big Cheese, the Head Po-Bahs, the Heavy-weights, the Big-Guns, the Big-shots, the High-Muckity-Mucks, the Big-Kahunas, the Head-Honchos, the Biggest Cones of all the Cone-Heads. They laid down the gauntlet and they've come back now to prove to humanity exactly who and what they are. They said they are immortal and can never die. They said that none of the Jews, Christians, or Muslims would be able to stand up against their superior Styoil [**43N**]:

He said, *'I am Prince Ea, I am my own master and there is none besides me, the gods of other planets and civilizations never saved them, what is this foolish trust you place in the supposed god of Abraham?'* < He said, *'I am Prince Ea, 'the god of Abraham' who you worship was merely the type and shadow my brother, Enki, and he will not save you: only I, Prince Ea can save you, and give you back the pure Adamic DNA'* He has challenged the Jews, Christians, and Muslims of earth. He says your God is no god at all, but only his brother or brothers, the type and shadow of Enki or Enlil. [43N] He said that Almighty God of the universe is merely another cone-head like himself. He said he formed the soul of mankind in an accidental genetic experiment gone wrong. [43N] He says you're just a cosmic space-monkey and you all should bow down and give service to his superior Styoil.

The Anunnaki represent a type of 3rd force here, neither beholden to The Galactic Federation of Worlds, nor to The Reptoid-Empire-Orion-Group. [A31] [12L] They are nevertheless super-big-dicks that literally claim to be God. [43N] To recap: The good news is there is actually a real Death-Star in our solar-system the size of a small moon often termed Nibiru, Planet X, or the Dark-Star in conspiracy circles. Which I think is actually kind of cool. The bad news is that rather than Darth Vader or Grand Moff Tarkin piloting it, the Anunnaki piloting it have stupid-looking heads and are super insecure about it, yet this technological terror is no match for the power of the dark-side.

We Dress up As Captain Picard and Dr. Beverley Crusher and Negotiate with the Pleiadean Delegation

"Perhaps it is a human failing; but we are not accustomed to these kinds of changes. I can't keep up. How long will you have this host? What would the next one be? I can't live with that kind of uncertainty. Perhaps, someday, our ability to love won't be so limited."

– Dr. Beverley Crush, from Star-Trek the Next Generation (1987-1994)

Leverage. In order to fully understand the situationship between us and the Space-Elf-Pleiadean Galactic-Federation people, we have to go back to High School. A bizarre series of events befell me then that I now know was but a preparation for this hour, and for this trial. As a teenager I was innocently minding my own business one day, sweeping leaves in my backyard as accomplishing a chore for my mom (who was out to lunch and a completely negligent single-parent as you will soon see) A young woman, 20s-30s something unexpectedly addressed me from the other side of the fence. She explained she was a piano-teacher and had grown intoxicated by the glorious sound-waves she heard emanating day after day from my prodigious musical compositional abilities on the pianoforte. Something like a warning wafted across my consciousness. The vibes from her were out-of-the-ordinary but not unpleasant. Plus, upon further examination between two fence-planks she was a bombshell. She had almost certainly donned the airy *Sound of Music* Fraulein-Maria summer-dress for the purpose, an odd choice for 90's silicon-valley, like she was supposed to be Julia Andrews from the *Sound of Music*. She knew what she was doing. She continued her attempted seduction by inviting me over to her place to experience the beauty of her perfectly-tuned grand-piano. I was somewhat naïve at the time. I give her an A++ for smoothness and subtlety. Over the next following months she precured for us a series of musical gigs at nursing homes, ministering to the inmates there. Thinking back this also skillfully had the additional benefit of making our seemingly large age-difference seem negligible. She was paying the long-game. She skillfully and subtly began to craft a visionary-future for both of us where we would one day end up becoming famous artists, composing sweet music together . . . forever. She was careful to offer a process forward, but not to violate my free-will in the process at any time, I believe out of a genuine love or regard. Eventually she began to invite me over for joint-meditation sessions replete with New Age music, indoor-fountains, yoga-mats surrounded by all her earth-mother-fertility-goddess idols. Just the two of us. No one else. This is basically also how the Space-Elves behave. This was the breaking point for me however, not in that I was particularly offended, but that in the final result I couldn't abandon my religion. This is somewhat like our situationship with the Space-Elves right now. Although I couldn't see it at the time, *I* actually held all the power in the relationship *because* I was the junior-partner. Because every genuine lover will never exploit the inexperience of their beloved, but rather kneel before it. I could have made her take me to Great America, or Santa-Cruz Beach Boardwalk, or Lake Tahoe. I could have demanded a $5,000 ring and a $10,000 wedding. I could have robbed her blind and she would have had very little recourse against it. It was only due to my inexperience that I failed to realize the true power-dynamics at work. That was the only reason I did not realize my power. She seemed older and wiser. At the time I was too pure-of-heart to contemplate such real-politics, but fortunately for you all and all of Holy Terra, subsequent trials and tribulations have since left me scarred both physically and mentally, leaving me warped into a cunning and vengeful sociopath, like Batman. Likewise, it is we the Terrans, despite or because of our inexperience that hold all the real power in our situationship with the Space-Elves/Pleiadeans/Galactic-Federation-of-Worlds people. And despite what it may seem, they probably need us far more than we need them. Mysteries of the Universe my friends . . . you are not going to learn from the honorable Dr. Michael Salla, Emissary Alex Collier, Emissary Elena Danaan, or any of the other New Age peace-creeps that regularly inhabit UFO conventions. *[And to you-know-who-you-are, wherever you are, I wish you all the best throughout all the waves of the multiverse]*

Now bearing everything in mind that we have learned, let us continue our exposition of how we may negotiate with the Space-Elves. As much as I loathe Pleiadean Pantheism (the religion they will claim is not a religion) their Space-Federation may still be used as a military power-balance against the Orion-Aliens with whom they are at war. They may be used like General George Washington used the French Navy. We had the Army, they had the Navy. The Americans didn't have a Navy, so we got the French to be our Navy for us until we could build our own. We have secret Space-Programs going on now building our own Space-Navy within US Space-Force, and US Navy-Space, **[12L] [A31]** the situation is not as it was in 1954.

As with the French-American alliance of 1778, today also we Americans (and Terrans) have the Army, the Pleiadeans have the (Space) Navy. Terra has now an extremely, abnormally-large, population of what most of the Alien factions view as the best available up-and-coming Violent/Aggressive/Milataristic/Super-Soldiers/Mercenaries/Infantry/Cannon-fodder. That is, we may not be exactly the smartest, most spiritual (in their view), or long-lived race, but most of the Alien groups view the basic stock-model of Terran, especially our young-men, especially Germans and Han Chinese, as the best cannon-fodder Infantry-shock-troops available in the known universe. This is due to our combination of basic characteristics. Our medium-level-intelligence, ability to follow orders, fast learning of basic military skills, fast maturation, high-birthrates, hyper-aggression, and short-lifespans not least amongst them. We also tend to be innovative, adaptable to different environments, and resourceful (kind of like Mac-Gyver, 1985-1992) or less charitably like rats or squirrels that can never be gotten rid of no matter what you do, they find a way, and pop out again next spring eating your birdseed (somehow). It is interesting to think about but the other Alien races are not the same way.

Here, I'll help you, imagine I'm the Terran Commander-in-Chief, I guess of the Americans in this thought-experiment, and you are like one of my chief advisors and we sit down with the French-like Pleiadean delegation at the negotiating table with several other high-ranking Americans. I'm wearing my Captain Picard uniform, and you are wearing your Doctor Beverly Crusher uniform just to kind of get in the spacey-mood. The Pleiadean delegation basically looks like teenage Swedish Olympic athletes in tight-fitting Star-Trek uniforms from the re-boot series. In reality each one of them is anywhere from 300 to 600 years old. They're super nice. We share some Terran cookies and lemonade together as an act of mutual bonding. They choak down some of our abominable earth-food and pretend to like it for diplomatic purposes, but in reality they are super condescending about American food, just like French-people.

Now let's try to understand the basic situation. They have all the high-tech spaceships and high-moral platitudes but lack the population, repro-ductive-rate, sex-drive, and killer-instinct to actually kill their enemies or fight and win their own wars, kind of like French people. They are losing the Galactic War against the Reptoids overall because they are too girly to fight and have a sparce population and the Reptoids are railroading them at every turn. This is the basic situation and they will gladly admit this and have already admitted this [A31] [12L] (although in slightly different terms that basically mean the same thing) I'm happy to debate with them about this if they don't like my characterization of the situation. We don't want them to die because they have all the sexy Pleiadean women and con-versely the Reptoids, their enemies, are total demonic jerks that you don't want to share a prison-cell with. Plus the Reptoids as the Pleiadean's main enemies have more-or-less puppet-mastered our planet for thousands of years through the secret-societies raising our taxes and inflating our cur-rencies so we can't pay for stuff and set up child-trafficking networks to suck their lifeforce, -so they all need to die anyway. Conversely, we the Terran-Americans, have millions of unemployed cow-tipping Bowhunter survivalists from the mid-west and sideways-shooting gunslingers from our inner-cities that were raised on Call-of-Duty and Halo whose highest aspiration is to become some sort of real-world equivalent of a Star-Ship-Trooper. We have the Infantry, they have the Space-Force. Nevertheless, our bloated populations of hundreds of millions also allows that a signif-icant portion of our best and brightest that played Wing-Commander and Dogfight-Elite on Steam growing up instead will also make good candidates to become Starfighter-pilots at least as good if not better than the Pleiadean starfighter pilots they already have. And we can provide an almost-practically infinite stream of this gold-platinum human-capital because we still have way too much unprotected heterosexual sex at young ages, hang out at the club and country-Western bars picking up women, and because our planet is a lush garden-planet growing fields of Wheat and Barley as opposed to say Venus or Mars or a thousand other worlds inhabited by Aliens that are mostly just rocks. For these reasons in reality the Pleiadean's need for our support is far greater than our need for their support. And that's why they are back here at our planet bugging us.

They open with some witty banter, followed by gracious and noble salutations, as Space-Elves usually do. Then we enter into negotiations. They really have an urgent need to get this Terran Starship-Trooper + Starfighter-Pilot program going before the Orion Empire completely just donkey-punches the remainder of their Federation into oblivion. They don't believe in killing their worst enemies in battle (I'm being serious here, this is what they actually believe) [A31] [12L] Instead they try to capture them alive and unharmed and send them to New-Age medita-tion-seminars (again, not a joke). [A31] Obedience to military orders in their chain-of-command is completely voluntary. (I wish that were a joke) [A31] It starts to become abundantly clear to the Terran-American delegation, especially the military-officers amongst us, as to why they are losing the Galactic War despite their much more advanced technologies.

As a first order-of-business at the top of the menu the Pleiadean delegation unilaterally demands a full nuclear disarmament of the American Nation as a non-negotiable prerequisite for any further negotiations. They offer this with the full moral certainty of an Evangelical Minister demanding abolition of the Tomahawk to a Native-American Tribe. The other members of the Terran-American delegation's head's explode with incredulity. At length, the Pleiadeans drift off talking about Gia and the mother-life-force that envelops the universe, that we are all connected, I belong to you, you belong to me, love is the answer, everything-is-everything, unintentionally revealing their long-term spiritual plans for earth and its denizens.

Me: "I didn't like the way you spoke to the honorable Dr. Salla, Commander Val-Thor. You're not in a military position to be all coy and play hard-to-get like a College-Cheerleader-Sorority-Girl. Give us the damn med-beds or pound sand. Not on the moon, not on Mars. Next time I see Dr. Salla he better look about 27. He better look younger than me. There better be about 1,000 med-beds at Tripler Army Medical Center in Honolulu in 6 months time or we'll Nuke to smithereens all your fancy starships illegally in orbit of our planet and blow up your chances of Holy Terra as an ally for the next thousand years . . . *is that what you want*? Maybe you won't be able to co-opt Earth the planet into your ghay Federation at all, maybe it will be opposed to you. Then you'll really get your asses handed to you by the Reptoids, Nebu-Greys, and the Nacht-Waffen. You guys are ghay. You are destined to lose. God is a real and terrifying patriarch regarding which you have an enormous oversight and an incredible hubris to speak at us and those of our Covenants about which you have no knowledge; especially when it is *you* that need *us* and not the other way around. MAJIC-12 already reverse-engineered most of the pertinent military-technology we needed, we are confident we can unravel the rest in time. We will conquer the Galaxy and exterminate the Reptoids and the Nacht-Waffen on our own without your help. And we're keeping our Nukes. We love our Nukes. Good day."

And so the Pleiadean delegation beams back up to the Starship Excelsior somewhat sullen, because that's basically what had happened when negotiating with President Eisenhower and the Terran-American delegation already over 70 years ago. So they go back to their Starship and kind of sit around at the Space-Bar sipping Space-Elf tea, kind of sad. But then one of them gets a great idea and transmits it via telepathy to the other Space-Elves, "Hey guys! That didn't go so great with the Terrans, but what if we jump in our Time-Machine and go back to yesterday and intercept the previous versions of ourselves before they go on their diplomatic mission yesterday, and then stop them, the previous version of ourselves I mean, but then we go instead and try the whole thing over again?" . . . "yeah! that's a great idea Arwen-Aldarion-Thor-Val!" (they really have crazy Space-Elf names like that) **[A31]** And so they all jump in their time-machine and go back to yesterday. [ok they probably don't actually have time-travel that is quite that accessible or works quite like that, but more just for the fun of the thought-experiment . . .] And on the way back one Space-Elf says to the other Space-Elf, "you know, the Terrans dream too much sometimes . . ." **[A31]**

So there we are again, me in my Captain-Picard uniform, and you in your Dr. Beverly Crusher uniform along with the other top Terran-American brass at the negotiating table again with the Pleiadeans in the 2nd iteration. This time they brought their own snacks to share because they didn't want to have to eat our cookies again. And so we eat their snacks instead, I imagine something like Elf-Lembas from *Lord of the Rings*. And we are able to compliment them on the tastiness of their food. (just like the French love to be complimented regarding their food)

Me in Captain-Picard Uniform: "I'm getting like crazy de-ja-vu here, Space-Elves, are you sure you guys didn't jump in your time machine tomorrow after a failed negotiation attempt with us and go back to yesterday, which is today, to try the whole thing over again?"

Them: "hemerrph . . ."

Me in Captain-Picard Uniform: "Whatever. Let's try it again then."

The greetings are a little bit more perfunctory this time as we have actually already done it before in the previous iteration.

Me in Captain-Picard Uniform: "Ok Val-Thor, how 'bout this: we can provide ya'll with a steady stream of over-zealous Call-of-Duty and Halo-suckled young-man nutcases from the Midwest and our inner-cities as Starship Troopers to act as Space Marines for your ships and they can really take a hurting to the Reptoids and the Nebu-Greys, and the Orion Empire and the Space-NAZIs, especially with Pleiadean armor, gear, and transport, and a combination of Pleiadean and Terran weapons, but on these conditions, most of which is for your own good: They will/must/shall be commanded by Terran Officers and NCOs underneath our own Rules of Engagement, i. e. we are not going to sit there like ya'll do and try to capture each and every Sentient Reptoid and Space-NAZI unharmed even as he is trying to fry us with a plasma rifle; we are going to fry him first and be damn well pleased about it. If for some reason the enemy throws down their weapons and surrenders, we will collect them and deliver them to your officers for peace-creep re-education as you love to do, as a punishment, because with the Reptoids and the Space-NAZIs if you are able to reeducate them into some kind of Buddhist Monk, that is indeed preferable to the rapacious demonic entity they were before. BUT our Star-Ship Trooper Regiments will retain their own Terran Jewish, Christian, and Muslim chaplains, just like we have now for the spiritual benefit of our own Troopers and their necessary and vital connection with the Cosmic Creator, our Patriarchal Almighty God, the personhood and sovereignty of whom you deny, but we believe in time that you will be persuaded by our example as to the truth of our Abrahamic religions, especially in this context. Are we getting anywhere?"

Them: "Why would you need Terran weapons at all, when our weapons are thousands of years more advanced?" says they.

Me in my Captain-Picard Uniform: "Because your weapons aren't even designed to kill, but only to stun in most cases, our weapons are more primitive, barbaric, and effective when in Terran hands; we will leave it to our Terran subordinate commanders and NCOs as to which loadout of Terran and/or Pleiadean weapons to use for a given operation or campaign, and to design the MTOE for our Terran Regiments, but our weapon-loadouts shall not be constrained by your ridiculous ethical standards. Are we getting anywhere?"

Them: ". . . but when you join the Galactic Federation of Worlds" says they, "you will have to abide by The Prime Directive and Federation instructions regarding Just War, Rules of Engagement, and the handling of Prisoners . . ."

"not so fast" says you and I in our StarFleet suits, "Who said anything about joining the Federation? This is a limited-term Military-alliance on a 5-year renewable contract, not forever, and not joining like that. I'm the dark-mirror image of Captain Picard, the real one, the bad one, not the nice lightside-one from the TV-series. Patrick-Stewart is just an actor. Plus you may view it as a pragmatic military-expedient that is necessary in this case: if the Terrans remain unconstrained by your overly-rigorous Federation Rules of Engagement, we might actually be able to do real damage to the Orion Empire, especially when coupled with certain elements of Pleiadean and Federation technology."

The Pleiadean delegation looks obviously worried by this proposition.

Yet I continue in my dark-mirror-verse Captain Picard Uniform: "In this regard the Terrans would represent a kind of grey-area 3rd Force that hasn't existed before, not like this. This may in fact be the solution to your dilemma that you have been searching for. The killer Terran Regiments and Starfighter-Pilots working for you may actually be able to defeat the Orion-Empire Reptoids, Greys, and Space-NAZIs who are too numerous and aggressive for you right now. You would be benefitted by the practically-unlimited manpower pipeline of zealous and resourceful Soldiers and Starfighter Pilots from Holy Terra, outfitted with the best and latest Pleiadean technologies would be formidable indeed. Your squeamish natures, small-populations, low-birthrates, slow-maturation, slow-learning, Impossible Rules of Engagement, unrealistic and wrong Ethical Standards, and generally Pacifist-deportment has severely limited your warfare capacity up until now. Terran Soldiers and Starfighter-Pilots fighting on your behalf would represent a solution to all these problems simultaneously. Moreover, Almighty God has maneuvered you into this position in order to teach you a lesson. In exchange for these benefits of potentially millions of Soldiers and Pilots you can give us protective forcefields for our major cities first; Med-Beds; Vrill-Energy infrastructure; and a host of other advancements."

Them: "But you will have to join the Federation if you want our full unmitigated military protection, and the benefits of our more advanced technologies" say they

"That's exactly it" says I, "we *don't* want your full unmitigated military protection which would surely include your New-Age Gurus new-ageing up the place. We want your protection and presence to be mitigated, very, very, mitigated. Kind of like how the Sudis treat Americans even when we have military bases there. Culturally, we are basically unable to penetrate their regressive culture. That's how we want it to be with you. With all your ghay-faggy ideas about peace-light-and-love kept at a distance, not to corrupt our youth. Our scriptures say, *'A time for peace and a time for war, a time to heal and a time to kill, a time to love and a time to hate'* this is balance, is it not? We bring balance to the Force in this regard, as you might say. In fact, your philosophy of always love, always peace, always heal, and never kill, never hate is in fact imbalanced, is it not? By your own definition it is the Terrans that are balanced capable of both light and dark energies, both love and hate, and it is in fact your people that are imbalanced. Isn't that why you are losing the war? You have lost the capacity to hate that which should be hated. The actions of the Reptoids and Orion-Greys and the Nacht-Waffen are hate-worthy, they have brought hate upon themselves by their actions, thus hate towards them in a military context is in fact Righteous, a RIGHTEOUS AEON, is this not so? You can help us with all kinds of logistics, medical treatments for our wounded Soldiers, Space-Marines, and Pilots, you can help us set up bases on other planets and moons and starfighter, carrier, and stardestroyer production facilities way faster than we would be able to do ourselves. But we can do most of the actual killing of the Orion-Group Reptoids, Greys, and Space-NAZIs, and probably most of the dying too. As long as our young men know they will be properly honored for their sacrifices and labor in a Righteous Cause they will be happy to do it. Most of our young men who are Jews, Christians, and Muslims have hope of the life-eternal in the higher planes with God anyway, and look forward to that as do I. This is your deep spiritual duty as it was in the beginning, to support us, on a deep level you know this to be true. *Search your feelings, You know this to be true.* This is the solution to your strategic-dilemma. The Reptoids and Orion-Greys beat you to the punch. They realized the implications of the emergence of mankind to the stars sooner than did you all, or at least they acted more swiftly, decisively, and more cunningly to develop Terran Pilots and Super-Soldiers during their intervention with the NAZIs and the Waffen-SS. Now we are playing catch-up. But you should also remember that it was mostly the Americans and Russians that defeated the NAZIs and the Waffen-SS in the last century on this planet anyway, forcing them to withdraw to Antarctica and off-world to other planets; they did not effect the full planetary takeover they were aiming for because of Americans. Now we are entering into a larger cycle. You are backed into a corner, I think. You don't want us to be Spacefaring as aggressive and militant and with the weapons we have now, and certainly not with a combination of Nukes and Pleiadean systems and weaponry, but you need our millions of Soldiers and Starfighter-Pilots from Terra on your side in the war. You had hoped to obscure these facts from us in order to retain negotiating-leverage, but Terrans also have a few prophets, seers, and Political-Scientists like me who perceive deeply. Be it known that I stand firmly by my precious predecessor and brother in Christ, Dr. Frank Strange, who although may not have been as perceptive, subtle, or well-versed in Cosmic matters, was nevertheless completely faithful to the Covenant of his God. You should perceive that I am a creature of the same department, or rather, a far worse exponent of this same soul-type, and my perceptive understanding of your wrongful doctrines does not indicate my inclination towards them, nor your Pantheistic religion-type with its errors (that you wrongfully claim is not a religion). In this scenario I believe it is best if Christian America negotiates with you in this way, as a type of Evangelical outreach, this is consistent with the spirit of Christianity. While Christian Russia remains independent, compartmentalized away from your insidious Pantheistic religion-type (that you wrongfully claim is not a religion). So that whatever spiritual damage you do to us over time in tempting us away from our Covenants, Chrisitan Russia will remain clear of and be able to rectify in the fullness of time. This is how we as the Terrans will be able to navigate this difficult passage. It will be difficult for you to fully corrupt 2 Billion Christians and another 2 Billion Muslims away from their Covenants. I do not think you will be able to do so, even though you must try."

The Pleiadeans are deeply disturbed by this lecture, enough to end the meeting this time of their own accord.

Space-Elves back at the Space Bar again . . . One Space-Elf to the other Space elf, "That deal with the Terrans didn't go so well, again."

"Hey guys, I have an idea! . . ."

The day before yesterday (again) me in my Captain Jean-Luc Picard outfit and you in your Dr. Beverly Crusher outfit sitting across from the Space-Elves again:

Them: "Many of you may feel a strong connection to us, that's because you *are* us, and a matter-of-fact many of you are cosmic star-seeds incarnated here at this very hour amongst the Terrans to . . ."

Me: "Shut up. I feel like we've been here forever, Val-Thor, going around in circles and we haven't even started yet . . . Allow me to consult with my team . . ."

We can also imagine this as a deal with a foreign Civilization like if we are playing Sid Meir's Civilization V:

Terrans will provide	in exchange for	Federation will provide
5-year renewable military alliance 1,000 strapping combat-ready Star-Ship-Troopers per year for front-line combat in Federation Wars (*but this number may be increased if they haggle for it)		5-year renewable military alliance
		#1 No ghay lectures from Space-Elves about the Galactic-Mother-Goddess. Federation shall immediately cease and desist all infiltration & subversion efforts of Jewish, Christian, & Muslim groups and other nativist religions
100 strapping combat-ready Terran Starfighter pilots per year for front-line combat in Federation Wars (*but this number may be increased if they haggle for it)		

		Assistance in production of a Star-Ship Enterprise USS Enterprise-D – equivalent with yours-truly standing in as Captain for Jean-Luc Picard (Patrick Stewart is just an actor)
		Father's visitation rights, Alimony for German men and other victims of Female Pleiadean abuses (Trust Men)
		1,000 operational Med-Beds at Walter Reed National Military Medical Center for Terran military-personnel
		1,000 operational Med-Beds at Standford Medical Center in Palo-Alto, California, for Citizen use

*the point is to drive a hard-bargain, don't let the Space-Elves sweet-talk us into giving away our shirts here

*If they don't agree to our terms we will threaten to go rouge and/or join the Reptoid-Empire. I think that this type of infantile, Kim-Jung-Un-esque brinkmanship should actually work quite well.

Cosmic Policy Solutions for Consideration

#1 Revocation of MAJIC-12's secret Treaties with The Orion Group

#2 Make the Galactic Federation of Worlds sign an agreement that they will cease and desist interference in our Terrestrial Religions; they will certainly break this in the future, they can't help themselves, but it would still be good to get it in writing.

#3 Negotiate with the Galactic Federation of Worlds to give us med-beds. This has the potential to alleviate a host of sufferings on this planet.

#4 Hold on to our Nukes as a Deterrent Force against all comers; they probably have a potential to blow up our planet, but that also means they have the potential to blow up other planets as well and lends an additional type of gravatas to our Diplomatic Corps. Ukraine gave up their Nukes and got invaded by Russia, we would be wise to examine the historical precedents here.

#5 Provide a certain number of "Starship Troopers", both as Space Marines and for Starfighter Pilots to the Galactic Federation of Worlds per year; this will aid them in their wars with the Orion Group and give our Soldiers and Pilots valuable experience. This concept may be tested with 1 initial "Starship Trooper" Regiment #1 of a thousand Soldiers for starters. I'm happy to volunteer as the CO, XO, S-3, S-2, or Alpha-Troop Commander for the expedition. If the model regiment is operationally successful in working with the Galactic Federation of Worlds, they may negotiate with us for X number of additional Regiments based on the original model Regiment. Supplied with a mix of Terran and Federation technologies combined. This is probably the answer to the Federation's current strategic military dilemma.

#6 Formation of an Anti-DNA corruption Task Force; Corruption of Adamic DNA violates Cosmic Law

#7 Release of Inventions of Nikolia Tesla from behind Governmental Control to General Public

#8 Detente with the Pleiadeans and Galactic Federation; but not join Federation; 5-year renewable military alliances only

#9 Detente with Russia and China, the other Planet Earth Superpowers, at least until the Alien Question gets sorted out.

#10 Full Assertion of our Planetary Rights to the Earth, the Moon, Mars, and all planets, planetoids, and objects orbiting Sol

#11 The Nacht Waffen Should be Given a Pathway to Redemption, Co-op some, kill the rest

#12 Zero-Point Energy Development; 'Vril' Energy is Real, Free, and Nikolai Tesla already discovered it over 100 years ago

Galactic Manifest Destiny

"No. I am your father."

. . .

"Let us rule the Galaxy as father and son!"
– Dather Vader to Luke Skywalker, Star Wars episode V,
The Empire Strikes Back

No matter what the Aliens do, mankind still goes spaceborne on any Timeline. And to be accurate, one must always prophesy the past. The human race has gone nuclear and spaceborne and the proverbial genie cannot be put back into the bottle. Mankind will prove to be fast-learners. The Pleiadeans will try to mitigate the situation through the spirit of the New Age Religion, that they will claim is not a religion. The Orion Group will try to mitigate the situation by pitting their Nacht-Waffen Super Soldiers against everyone else in the universe, thereby partially coopting the destiny of at least a part of the human race. On earth, the influence of The Orion Group will shortly be routed in near-decades, along with their human collaborators, with Pleiadean and Galactic Federation help. Many crimes uncovered. Despite Outer-Space foes the various human factions and countries will still continue to compete against and invade one-another for dominance of the Earth, Moon, Mars, and beyond with Outer-Space Aliens of various factions being permanent fixtures in international and intergalactic politics. The Solar-System and Planet Earth will suffer several counter-attacks by The Orion Group in following decades and centuries in attempts to recapture it, but these will not be successful.

For their part the Pleiadeans will try to get the largest coefficient of planet earth to join in their mutual-defense alliance, The Galactic Federation of Worlds. Part of the Earthlings will want to join, and part will not want to join. To this end the Pleiadeans and the Galactic Federation of Worlds will try to foster as many good-vibes and close-ties with the Earthlings as possible. The Pleiadean influence on earth will become enormous, through cultural, spiritual, scientific, and religious efforts that Christian and Muslim fundamentalists will attempt to expel in vain. This will lead into and synchronize with what many Christians and Muslims will view as end-times events prophesied by their respective holy-books. Additionally, the New Age Ascended Masters of the Intergalactic Confederation of worlds, at a higher plane, will stoop to occupy Anti-Christ roles on earth over the next 1,000 years that will be resisted by fundamentalist Jews, Christians, and Muslims for a time.

Spirituality, far from being quashed by Alien Contact, will be amplified a thousand-fold as mankind awakens to the larger multi-verse in a new paradigm. Especially the Pleiadean peoples, bringing with them the spirit of the New Age Religion from an advanced spacefaring civilization, will have a tidal-wave impact on the spirituality and religions of Earth. They will be viewed as Heroes of Light and Love with an every-increasing presence and influence over Earth and her peoples a thousand times more impactful and long-lasting than the short, negative Orion-Group influence the Earth has experienced over the last 100 years. Atheism, having been scientifically disproven by the Pleiadeans, will have to roll any of its remains into New Age Pantheism.

The New Age Religion on Earth, that they will claim is not a religion, is amplified a thousand-fold by the Pleiadeans and the Galactic Federation of Worlds, in addition to the doctrines of the New Age Ascended Masters of the Intergalactic Confederation of a higher plane, the Andromedans. The New Age Religion will become much more prominent and common-place on the earth, and will come into stark opposition with 2 Billion Christians, and 2 Billion more Muslims. Of the two, the Muslims will be the more resistant to its charms, and serve as an unexpected support to Christianity during the period of its vexation by the spirit of the New Age. Yet, the spirit of the New Age will succeed in warping a portion of the Christians and a portion of the Muslims to their aims, within the context of a Panthianatized Christianity and a Pantheanatized Islam. This external off-word pressure from the spirit of the New Age will have the unintended consequence of pushing Traditional Islam into more close alignment with Traditional Judeo-Christianity, each of which will become more radicalized even as they come into more common terms with each other in successive generations. In 100 years it will be almost impossible for successive generations to understand the difference between Judaism and Christianity, the worst fears of Traditionalists in both religions being realized. In 500 years the result will be a kind of Judeo-Chrislam, a type of synergistic re-unification of the Earthly Abrahamic faiths. Anticipating this, the Andromedans will have will launched initiatives to coopt the reunification. Thus, there will be a Right and Left Wing of Judeo-Chrislam, or Monotheistic vs. Pantheistic sides to the new synergy of the three Abrahamic Faiths.

Nevertheless, renewed interest in and greater availability of the Book of Enoch and understanding into the pre-diluvian world shall result in a kind of Enochian-Metatron-Judeo-Chrislam, a culmination of planet Earth's Covenants with the Cosmic Creator. A kind of spiritual-synergy of the Crusader and the Mujahadeen armed with Nukes. Similar to Joshua and Caleb entering the promised-land, or Mohammad's wars of conquest in Arabia, the very worst fears of most other peaceful civilizations being realized. Somewhat cowed, and in a state-of-mind similar to what we now call Stockholm-Syndrome, some of the Pleiadeans, especially the women Pleiadeans, will adopt Christianity and/or Islam, simultaneously as a kind of reverse-infiltration effort, even as many more Earthlings are adopting the spirit of the New Age due to the cultural mix of all factions.

Controversies over the Christian Apostle Paul introduced by Muslim hatred of the man will escalate into full-scale religious wars, somewhat comparable to the Catholic vs. Protestant Wars of Religion in Europe in the 1500s. Yet this will not be a strictly Muslim vs. Christian conflict as before: Half of the Christians shall reject him and Half shall retain him; the half that reject him shall come into alliance with the Muslims and the Jews, and thus being superior in number shall gain the upper hand. Thus, the selection of the books of the bible will change with the Epistles being thrown out and the books of Enoch being added back in. Christians will revert to Old Testament Law and the Apocalypse of John, yet the Gospels shall be retained. Christians shall move into a new understanding of Islam similar to their reproachment with Judaism which began in the second-half of the 1900s. This will occur even as the spirit of the New Age will metastasize into what many Christians, Muslims, and Jews will view as particular fulfillments of their various end-times prophesies. There will be several iterations of events throughout different centuries that both Christians, Muslims, and Jews will perceive as being fulfillments of prophesy regarding The Antichrist and the Mark of the Beast. These religio-political conflicts will continue for thousands of years into the future with only brief periods of peace between successive rounds of conflict, strife, and war due to these ideological, theological, and cosmological differences that will not be able to be mitigated by anyone and no part of the journey will be easy to navigate by any of the participants.

The Galactic Federation of Worlds and the spirit of the New Age that underpins them will remain a lasting fixture in all these events. They will not all be converted to Christianity, nor to a monotheistic religion, nor will they all be displaced, but their final judgement shall be prolonged yet again to unto a future age; they shall enjoy a long continuance of their body-politic and institutions; the only difference in the near-future being a parallel coexistence with spacefaring human civilizations, some of which will be Abrahamic in character. Further in time the Earthlings will guard the Pleiadeans and the Galactic Federation of Worlds peoples from attacks by demonic beings from the lower planes. The Culmination of the Earthling Abrahamic Covenants shall represent a stark challenge and opportunity for reconciliation with the Cosmic Creator, especially to the Pleiadeans who have the most close-contacts with the Earthlings. Some of the Pleiadeans, will revert from Pantheism to a type of Monotheism akin to Christianity; yet being in a very small minority of their people, these views they will keep mostly to themselves, yet this mechanism shall allow some of the Pleiadeans reconciliation with God and to incarnate back unto the higher planes.

Mankind shall prove to be fast-learners. Due to new pressures Terrans will evidence additional abilities both psychic and physical even without the aid of technology. These latent developing psychic and physical abilities shall be comparable with, and in some cases exceeding the abilities that other Extraterrestrial Species and individuals already possess. Despite, or perhaps because of their short life-spans, the Terrans shall prove themselves adaptable and enterprising in Space; with a multitude of new Terran factions, groups, nations, and corporate entities exploring and colonizing many other worlds. Descendants of the Russians, Chinese, Japanese, Americans, Scandinavians, Lockheed-Martin, and the Waffen-SS among others shall colonize many other worlds and come into stark conflict with each-other and many other peaceful civilizations and Species. Like herding cats, this situation shall prove difficult for the already-entrenched Galactic Empires to control despite their advanced technologies. At the zenith of their problem-causing the Terrans shall push The Galactic Federation of Worlds and the Reptoid-Empire into detente in order to deal with the Terran problem; but this will not last long. The Terrans shall prove highly adept at technology-theft of other civilizations and reverse-engineering. Many Terrans shall have their already short-lives cut even shorter by Alien retaliatory-attacks at something like a 2 to 1 ratio with the Terrans getting the worst of it; as in 2 Terrans killed for every 1 Alien. However, due to creativity, fast learning, high reproduction rates, and fast maturation amongst the Terrans, the Terran infestation of the Galaxy shall never fully be cured.

The end result will be various human-descended groups taking up residence on all kinds of different planets and moons throughout the Galaxy, with descendants of Germans, Americans, Russians, Chinese and others all having representation, and becoming major intergalactic-contenders along with and putting military and political pressure on The Orion Group,

The Galactic Federation of Worlds, the Anunnaki peoples, and others, and displacing some of them. The human vendetta and blood-feud against The Orion Group will be intense due to their actions on planet earth in the 20th and 21st centuries that will become fully exposed and not soon forgotten. In this manner the age-old battle between man and serpent shall continue, with mankind routing and excoriating many a world of the Reptoid presence, neither will the Zeta Reticuli be forgotten as part of the vendetta and blood-feud due to their participation. Yet the Galactic Federation of Worlds will avoid the greater part of mankind's militancy, having intentionally sown positive-Karma early-on, and looking far ahead, yet the ideological conflicts of Pantheist vs. Monotheist shall continue forever.